How Entrepreneurs Do What They Do

How Entrepreneurs Do What They Do

Case Studies in Knowledge Intensive Entrepreneurship

Edited by

Maureen McKelvey

Professor of Industrial Management, School of Business, Economics and Law, University of Gothenburg, Sweden

Astrid Heidemann Lassen

Associate Professor of Innovation Management, Center for Industrial Production, Aalborg University, Denmark

Edward Elgar

Cheltenham, UK • Northampton, MA, USA

Published by
Edward Elgar Publishing Limited
The Lypiatts
15 Lansdown Road
Cheltenham
Glos GL50 2JA
UK

Edward Elgar Publishing, Inc.
William Pratt House
9 Dewey Court
Northampton
Massachusetts 01060
USA

A catalogue record for this book
is available from the British Library

Library of Congress Control Number: 2012949256

This book is available electronically in the ElgarOnline.com Business Subject Collection, E-ISBN 978 1 78100 550 7

ISBN 978 1 78100 549 1

Typeset by Columns Design XML Ltd, Reading
Printed and bound by MPG PRINTGROUP, UK

Contents

Figures

Tables

Contributors

Ann-Sofie Axelsson, PhD, Associate Professor, Department of Technology Management and Economics, Chalmers University of Technology, Sweden.

Rudi Bekkers, PhD, Assistant Professor, School of Innovation Sciences, Eindhoven University of Technology, Netherlands.

Luca Bordoli, Research Trainee, Department of Business and Management, Aalborg University, Denmark.

Johan Brink, PhD, Senior Lecturer, Institute for Innovation and Entrepreneurship, School of Business, Economics and Law, University of Gothenburg, Sweden.

Oskar Broberg, PhD, Associate Professor, Department of Economy and Society, School of Business, Economics and Law, University of Gothenburg, Sweden.

Manuel Mira Godinho, PhD, Professor of Economics, UECE and ISEG – School of Economics and Management, Technical University of Lisbon, Portugal.

Jens Laage-Hellman, PhD, Associate Professor, Chalmers University of Technology and Institute for Management of Innovation and Technology (IMIT), Sweden.

Astrid Heidemann Lassen, PhD, Associate Professor, Center for Industrial Production, Department of Business and Management, Aalborg University, Denmark.

Daniel Ljungberg, PhD, Postdoc Researcher, Institute for Innovation and Entrepreneurship, School of Business, Economics and Law, University of Gothenburg, Sweden.

Ricardo Mamede, PhD, Assistant Professor, Department of Political Economy, ISCTE-University Institute of Lisbon, Portugal.

Maureen McKelvey, PhD, Professor of Innovation and Industrial Management, Institute for Innovation and Entrepreneurship, School of Business, Economics and Law, University of Gothenburg, Sweden.

Christian Richter Østergaard, PhD, Associate Professor, Department of Business and Management, Aalborg University, Denmark.

Eunkyung Park, PhD Candidate, Department of Business and Management, Aalborg University, Denmark.

Alexandra Rosa, PhD Candidate, Social Sciences Department, School of Economics and Management, Technical University of Lisbon, Portugal.

Gustav Sjöblom, PhD, Postdoc, Department of Technology Management and Economics, Chalmers University of Technology, Sweden.

Dmitrij Slepniov, PhD, Assistant Professor, Center for Industrial Production, Department of Business and Management, Aalborg University, Denmark.

Stefan Szücs, PhD, Associate Professor, CEFOS – Center for Public Sector Research, University of Gothenburg, Sweden.

Bram Timmermans, PhD, Postdoc Researcher, DRUID -IKE/EOB, Department of Business and Management, Aalborg University, Denmark.

Brian Vejrum Waehrens, PhD, Associate Professor, Center for Industrial Production, Department of Business and Management, Aalborg University, Denmark.

Olof Zaring, PhD, Senior Lecturer, Institute for Innovation and Entrepreneurship, School of Business, Economics and Law, University of Gothenburg, Sweden.

Yanmei Zhu, PhD, Vice Dean, Associate Professor, School of Economics and Management, Tongji University, China.

Preface and acknowledgement

This book is dedicated to Ingemar Broman, a Scholar of the School of Business, Economics and Law, University of Gothenburg, Sweden. He was a valued financial adviser and a very successful trader. He generously donated most of his fortune to the School. The Broman Foundation is used to support research in the area of innovation and entrepreneurship. Ingemar would have been delighted to see how well his wealth has been used so far to stimulate interesting research and practical applications.

This book is developed in a larger context in relation to the AEGIS project – 'Advancing Knowledge Intensive Entrepreneurship and Innovation for Economic Growth and Social Well-being in Europe', which is the European Union 7th Framework project AEGIS, project contract number 225134. AEGIS aims to examine knowledge intensive entrepreneurship (KIE), its defining characteristics, boundaries, scope and incentives in high-technology as well as low-technology sectors and services. The reports from this project are freely available, and constitute many papers with interesting results and insights about KIE. We encourage the reader of this book to also seek out such knowledge at http://www.aegis-fp7.eu.

1. Introduction

Maureen McKelvey and Astrid Heidemann Lassen

1.1 INTRODUCTION

How Entrepreneurs Do What They Do presents 13 case studies of
knowledge intensive entrepreneurship. The book focuses on what we call
'doing', meaning what happens when entrepreneurs are engaging practically in venture creation processes.

The case studies cover a broad range of different types of firms, in
different sectors and distributed around the globe. The reason being that
this type of entrepreneurship can be found in many sectors and countries.
The cases range from low-tech industries like food, to design firms like
advertising, through service firms like software, and also high-tech
sectors like biotechnology and pharmaceuticals. The cases are grouped
into the broad headings of 'Transversal technologies, engineering and
software', 'Lifestyle technologies' and 'Human health care and food'.

These cases as well as a companion conceptual book focus on
knowledge intensive entrepreneurship, which is shortened to KIE. They
describe and define KIE as a particular type of start-up venture and
phenomena. Their business models and organizational forms are particularly dependent upon the intersection of different types of knowledge,
including three types discussed in the cases. They include (1) the
scientific, technological and creative knowledge, which helps produce
novel ideas; (2) the market knowledge, which relates to an understanding
of customers and potential markets and (3) the business knowledge,
which is related to running the venture and firm. Given the level of
novelty involved, the market often needs to be 'created' rather than
already existing.

Entrepreneurship can refer to both the persons and the phenomena, so
this book uses some consistent definitions. The individual person and
team who start the venture are called entrepreneur and founder. We use
the term 'KIE venture' for the company, business project or new

organizational form created in this way. The KIE venture may have significant linkages to the previous organizations where the founder worked, like universities or large existing companies. So to highlight these linkages, the ventures can be labelled as 'academic spin-offs' and 'corporate spin-offs' or they may be started by independent inventors and creative individuals.

Each case has been chosen to illustrate specific aspects in the different phases of a venture creation, and is related to the KIE model. This includes renewal through KIE ventures that are small companies. But some cases also follow the actions of larger organizations, usually firms, to develop new organizational forms and meeting points, in order to manage the challenges of innovation such as the need to access the Chinese market and information or the need to renew traditional industries like food.

All cases also demonstrate how and why the actual doing of this type of entrepreneurship rarely confirms to standard solutions or strict business planning. Instead, taken together, these 13 cases show that the phenomena of KIE are achieved through a series of decisions, which lead to the balancing of alternative logics between business planning and the emergence of unexpected opportunities.

Most chapters focus upon individuals and KIE ventures, but they also link to the broader context of the innovation system, such as networks, industrial dynamics and the role of universities or large firms in stimulating innovation. These ventures are highly linked to their ecosystem and external environment, especially for accessing resources and ideas but also understanding their potential users and market. Therefore, the chapters may also use the concept of KIE for this overall phenomenon of entrepreneurship. This captures these broader dynamics.

The next section presents our KIE model, including the key processes and variables involved in this particular type of entrepreneurship. The concluding section introduces each case study.

1.2 CASES STUDIES IN RELATION TO THE KIE CONCEPTUAL MODEL

Understanding the KIE model and phenomena should enable the reader to use them as a knowledge platform for learning about, engaging in and evaluating performance. The reader interested in the details of the KIE conceptual model is referred to *Managing Knowledge Intensive Entrepreneurship* (McKelvey and Lassen, 2013).

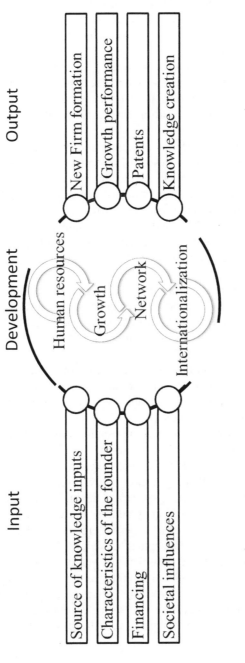

Figure 1.1   The KIE conceptual model

The KIE model is firstly useful to place the 13 case studies in context, in terms of phases and variables of this type of entrepreneurship.

Figure 1.1 provides a visualization to facilitate the discussions and details of the model and of the special characteristics and starting points of this type of entrepreneurship.

The first phase we consider in the conceptual framework of KIE addresses accessing resources and ideas: inputs to KIE ventures. Four related variables are included as particularly crucial: financing, character-istics of founder, sources and endowments and the influence of institu-tional forces.

The second phase concerns managing and developing the KIE venture. This phase refers to the processes of managing and developing KIE. This is largely an internal process, referring to the internal competences, resources and approaches affecting the management and growth of the new venture after initial formation. However, many of these variables require interaction with the external environment, but the combination of knowledge and internal and external processes and organizations is what results in the designing of opportunities and their realization through business models.

The third and final overall phase is related to evaluating performance and outputs. This discussion focuses upon the different types of outcome generated through KIE, and more broadly, the effects of this output on economic growth and social well-being as well as how to measure performance and outputs.

Another way to summarize how the KIE conceptual model leads us to stress certain aspects in the case studies (Table 1.1).

Table 1.1 thus illustrates the topics and types of data that will be used to understand our case studies.

Of course, writing a case study is usually more complex than depicted in a model. The point of a conceptual model is to clarify the key descriptive variables and if possible, explain the relationships between variables over time. Writing a case study involves, in contrast, what is sometimes called 'the messy empirical reality'. By that, we mean that one and the same case study may address multiple variables and phases, due to the complexity of these types of processes. Thus, another way of understanding the KIE conceptual model as found in Figure 1.1 and Table 1.1 is to understand how the KIE venture is involved in designing and the realization of innovative opportunities as a design process. By viewing KIE as a design process we are able to understand how the dynamic interactions between the variables outlined in the conceptual model are proactively approached and utilized by entrepreneurs, and that

Table 1.1 Key aspects found in case studies

Accessing resources and ideas	• Opportunity recognition • Characteristics and traits of founder(s) • Founding team composition • Knowledge bases • Human resources • Financial resources • Social resources • Institutional influences
Managing and developing the KIE venture	• Opportunity development • Managing transitions • Application of resources to growing the firm • Differential growth patterns • Decision-making and strategies • Continuing to access resources and ideas • External networks • Internationalization and globalization
Evaluating performance and outputs	• Financial data • Sales, performance, employment • Innovation in products, services and organizational forms • Social impacts • Knowledge spillovers to other firms or to society • Patterns of regional development

the ability to do so is an inherent part of KIE. This means that the managing and developing processes usually involve goals, planning and decision-making but they also involve changing those goals, adapting and learning as the firms understand new aspects of their knowledge and the environment around them. As such, competitive advantage in KIE ventures often arises emergently as a result of particular operating circumstances surrounding the enterprise. Here strategic management becomes primarily an adaptive and reflective process concerned with manipulating a limited amount of resources. The efforts are not concentrated on predicting or controlling the operating environment, but on adapting as quickly as possible to the changing demands of this environment.

Each case study tells a complex history, usually involving a chronological story-telling of what happens over time. In all cases, the firm has to adapt and change over time – usually dependent upon a combination of internal capabilities and ideas with external opportunities and networks. That is the reality facing entrepreneurs. However, to make the cases useful and interesting, each chapter defines a set of questions and provides answers through the case studies. This approach allows each case study to focus upon somewhat different issues, which may cross several dimensions of the model per se.

1.3 STRUCTURE OF THE BOOK

The book is entitled *How Entrepreneurs Do What They Do* because the chapters represent real case studies, as the KIE ventures change and develop over a series of years. The case studies involve firms located in different places globally, and many also work across national boundaries.

1.3.1 How the Case Studies were Chosen and Written

Each chapter illustrates how processes within the KIE conceptual model presented above work in detail. The structure of each chapter also relates the case study to concepts. Each is easy to read, and written according to the same structure, involving four sections. Each chapter poses a few questions, found in the introduction. These questions are addressed throughout the case study descriptions, and also summarized, followed by questions for further development of the ideas.

In telling these stories, the phases in the model are intertwined but so are the types of knowledge valuable to the venture. It is not always easy to tell, either, where the scientific, technological or creative knowledge stops and where the market and business knowledge starts. Indeed, many case studies demonstrate that initially the KIE venture thought that the scientific and technology knowledge was useful in one area, only to find its market application in a different industry or product.

Organizational forms are somewhat varied. The chapters primarily address the founding of independent ventures, but some chapters deal with more than that, because industries and countries differ. Some chapters include large firms and industrial dynamics. The reason for including them is that industrial and national contexts differ, and some are more conducive to starting small companies than other contexts. Thus, while case studies are intended to illustrate more general dimensions of KIE phenomena, some of them refer to the importance of the industrial and national context (or innovation system) when directly relevant.

Therefore, due to the differential nature of innovative opportunities in different industries and countries, the book also includes cases where the large firms are working to innovate – usually through interactions with KIE ventures or universities or starting their own subsidiaries. In some industries, not so many new firms are started, but the processes of renewal may be similar in terms of starting up new organizational forms – albeit as subsidiaries of larger companies – and so certain parts of the KIE conceptual model are applicable.

Most of the KIE ventures studied are anonymous. Two cases that address the history of the evolution of the whole industry are not anonymous, due to the large amount of data gathered involving company names. That gave us reason to include the real names of these sets of firms. Our rationale for keeping the firm names anonymous are for other reasons, for example, to keep the reader focused upon the analysis of what is going on, and the main lessons learned, rather than to try to familiarize himself or herself with the specific company.

Three broad sectors have been used to group the case studies, namely 'Transversal technologies, engineering and software', 'Lifestyle technologies' and 'Human health care and food'. The reason is to help demonstrate that there is a broad range of highly relevant sectors, and that these technologies may lead to further development of products or services in different, unexpected sectors.

1.3.2 Case Studies in Transversal Technologies, Engineering and Software

Transversal technologies, engineering and software refer to technologies that are useful across a range of applications or uses, and they also represent sectors in the economy. These technologies are often possible to adapt to different products and services. But at different levels of aggregation, they could be classified as high tech, low tech or medium tech. Economists looking at the industrial level would classify the firms into these three categories, depending upon the industrial average of sales invested into research and development (R&D). In these types of classifications, engineering industries are often classified as low or medium tech. Business economists, however, would look at the firms, and see that many of the firms could be classified as high tech, due to the fact that the firms use advanced technologies and hire highly educated employees. Thus, many of the cases in this book are dependent upon scientific and technological knowledge, even if economists would consider these industries as rather medium- to low-tech ones.

We find this discrepancy (or difference) in perspective, which arises due to the level of analysis, to be quite interesting and relevant to understanding KIE. It also has implications for which types of firms and industries to stimulate through public policy and to focus upon when starting a business. The reason is that using scientific and technological knowledge to renew industries and to develop new products and services can occur across the board. Indeed, one of the meanings of 'transversal technologies' is that they can be applied to many uses, which for the firm translates into many different categories of users, and of relevant products and services. This renewal through higher value services and products can occur through innovation in larger firms as well as through KIE ventures.

Renewing industrial leadership in this sense is often also related to new ways to innovate in large firms, but also to develop KIE ventures. The focus should be on moving from low value products and services to high value ones, and often by using scientific and engineering knowledge to renew the more traditional industries.

The five case studies of KIE ventures within Part I discuss technologies that may find many applications or uses. Several illustrate that a key issue for the KIE venture is to decide which users and markets could currently, or potentially, be relevant. These five cases also illustrate the interrelated nature of decision-making inside the firm with regard to developing markets, finding financing and developing the technologies in directions relevant to find new products and services.

Chapter 2 is entitled 'How tensions between exploration and exploitation drive the development process of KIE: the case of Sensor Inc.' and is written by Astrid Heidemann Lassen. This chapter explores how and why KIE ventures deal with the tensions and differing logics between technological knowledge, market knowledge and business knowledge. Sensor Inc. is initially heavily reliant upon specialist technological knowledge, and gradually moves into production and sales. This move requires changes in strategy, management practices, human resources and network collaborations, and financing sources alike. Such changes are experienced as tensions due to differences in focus, skills and priorities from both the founders of the venture, the human resources base of the venture and the external stakeholders. The key message of the chapter is that managing the KIE venture requires setting up organizational processes and management practices to allow the shifting foci. Moreover, an important driving force in the development of the venture includes these attempts to manage and address the tensions between exploitation and exploration.

The results of the chapter help us understand the interrelatedness of several of the variables illustrated in the KIE conceptual model (McKelvey and Lassen, 2013). The reason is that the case study illustrates how KIE is achieved through a series of decisions, which lead to the balancing of alternative logics between business planning and the emergence of unexpected opportunities. This supports the understanding of KIE as an iterative process of integration between variables affecting the founding of KIE ventures, variables affecting the management and growth of KIE ventures and variables measuring output of KIE in different dimensions.

Chapter 3 is entitled 'Collaborative strategies: how and why academic spin-offs interact with engineering university centers' and is written by Maureen McKelvey, Daniel Ljungberg, Olof Zaring, Jens Laage-Hellman and Stefan Szücs. This chapter follows the management and development of two KIE ventures that are academic spin-offs, in relation to collaborative strategies. The perspective is on how and why academic spin-offs continue to engage in collaborative strategies with engineering centres located at the university. The KIE ventures use the centres to access scientific and technological knowledge, as expected, but they are also interested in accessing other resources and networks to help further develop their research, product and market development. The key message is that networks with research centres at the university help shape the venture. Even after the founding phase, these KIE ventures can use collaborative strategies for research to access resources and ideas – involving scientific and technological knowledge but also market and business knowledge.

The results of the chapter help us understand in particular how the venture needs to continue to access resources and ideas, even during the management and development phase of the KIE conceptual model (McKelvey and Lassen, 2013). The KIE ventures are academic spin-offs, heavily involved in the development of technologies, and yet they greatly benefit from these university networks to access market knowledge from other established firms, and to access business knowledge through the recruitment of experienced managers.

Chapter 4 is entitled 'Interaction as a strategy in knowledge intensive entrepreneurship: the case of an ERP software company' and is written by Olof Zaring. This chapter illustrates how managing growth in an entrepreneurial enterprise is about balancing ups and downs, over time, which arise due to uncertainty in market conditions, technology and the supply of risk capital well beyond the initial founding of the venture. The case study follows a software company longitudinally over a 20-year period, and it demonstrates that growth of such a venture might well follow a non-linear process that defies original planning efforts. Hence, business planning becomes secondary to flexibility within the management team. The key message of the chapter is that the successful management during expansion and consolidation in KIE ventures may be a prolonged process requiring financial as well as management stamina and flexibility, where a company develops products, expands its market reach and faces crisis.

The results of the chapter help us understand the dynamics of KIE illustrated in the KIE conceptual model (McKelvey and Lassen, 2013), especially the processes. These uncertainties in market conditions, technology and the supply of risk capital lead to different ways of trying to manage the venture. Even as the KIE venture grows and matures, it may be facing dynamic external conditions that place continuous demands for adaptability, renewal and change.

Chapter 5 is entitled 'Managing international expansion in a KIE venture: going global in Alpha Composites' and is written by Dmitrij Slepniov and Brian Vejrum Waehrens. The case describes an international expansion of a small high-tech company seeking to apply its knowledge resources globally, despite its lack of international operations experience and scarce managerial resources. By exploring the process of green-field production start-up in China, the case illustrates many of the considerations behind how to best exploit the international opportunities related to highly specialized technical knowledge. The key message of the case is that the actual internationalization process of KIE seems to unfold in different ways and for different reasons than those normally found in international business theory. Furthermore, the case study shows how KIE is not restricted to new ventures, but can also be a process of organizational change in larger companies, which reflects the continuous pursuit of innovative opportunities by established firms.

The results of the chapter are related to the development phase of the KIE conceptual model (McKelvey and Lassen, 2013), which argues that internationalization of KIE is often brought on by the search for new opportunities, access to new knowledge and access to new markets.

Chapter 6 is entitled 'The nexus between technology, organizational and market development: the case of NanoSpace Inc.' and is written by Astrid Heidemann Lassen. This chapter explores how KIE ventures develop under conditions of technological, market and organizational uncertainty and immaturity. The case follows the development and gradual growth of NanoSpace Inc. This KIE venture develops, produces and sells nano-satellites, which are a new product. This implies that they have to work simultaneously on the development of the technology, the identification and development of possible applications or products, and the development of customers and ways to sell through market mechanisms. In particular, the market is immature and much uncertainty remains about possible applications and products. This is, on the one hand, a serious challenge in relation to growth, but, on the other hand, enables creative ways of collaborating in networks. The key message of the chapter is that network collaboration is imperative for KIE ventures, even one highly oriented towards technology, and these networks are built and utilized in a variety of manners.

The results of the chapter help us understand in particular the variables of the KIE conceptual model (McKelvey and Lassen, 2013), which address the development and growth phase of KIE. The case study shows how the business venture and the external ecosystem are dynamically related to one another in different ways and through different types of knowledge exploration and exploitation.

1.3.3 Case Studies in Lifestyle Technologies

Lifestyle technologies represent firms and industries involving technologies that are used in and help develop the modern society. In the digital society, many people invest in lifestyle and experiences, which are generally facilitated by information technology (IT) and telecommunications. Such contemporary technologies offer more flexible forms of social and economic activity, whereby the advanced nations begin exhibiting lifestyle-led and leisure-oriented development of the society. These sectors represent a growing part of many economies, largely because people are willing to change lifestyles, spend significant resources on hobbies, and this leads to shifts in consumer behaviour. Many of these aspects relate to societal well-being and lifestyle in the use of these technologies and ideas, although they may also represent significant segments of an economy.

The three cases in Part II represent fairly different types of sectors as related to lifestyle. In different ways, they demonstrate how endowments as well as access to resources and ideas impact not only the founding of one venture, but also the later development and management phases. In particular, all three chapters address how resources and ideas are transferred to other KIE ventures at a later stage, which leads to interesting observations about how and why KIE ventures affect the external environment, over time. In one case, the exit of a global large firm from a region opens up opportunities for new KIE ventures, while in another case, the exit of a KIE venture opens up opportunities for the individual founders to move to a global large firm. This suggests that interesting relationships exist between individuals, KIE ventures and large firms in ways that impact the external environment and the propensity or likelihood for new KIE ventures to start.

Chapter 7 is entitled 'Knowledge intensive entrepreneurship from firm exit in a high-tech cluster: the case of the wireless communications cluster in Aalborg, Denmark' and is written by Christian Richter Østergaard and Eunkyung Park. This chapter explores how the existence of a cluster of firms with a specific knowledge base in a region affects future KIE in that region. The chapter addresses what happens to the regional knowledge base in the wake of declining cluster activity, specifically when large global firms leave the region due to global crisis. The case study takes its point of departure in the decline of a once highly successful wireless communication cluster in Northern Denmark. It demonstrates how the decline does not mean the end of wireless communication ventures in the region, but rather the decline may spur new types of KIE ventures.

The results of the chapter reflect on several points related to the output variables of the KIE conceptual model (McKelvey and Lassen, 2013). The results demonstrate that KIE outputs cannot be adequately measured only in terms of absolute amounts (for example, number of firms in a cluster). Instead, a more accurate measure of output could be assessed through analysis of the types of jobs created and through analysis of the knowledge diffusion into new areas. The knowledge that is the output of one stage of KIE may lead to an input, and renewed start up of KIE ventures in a later stage, and they may even be stimulated in other industrial sectors.

Chapter 8 is entitled 'Entrepreneurial exploitation of creative destruction and the ambiguity of knowledge in the emerging field of digital advertising' and is written by Oskar Broberg, Ann-Sofie Axelsson and Gustav Sjöblom. The case study addresses how KIE in service firms is affected by the fact that knowledge is an uncertain asset, and it explores how ambiguity often arises in terms of technology, business and market potentials alike. The case traces the professional history of two individuals from the early 1990s up until 2010, and demonstrates how they, through their actions and interactions during their careers, handle the elusive knowledge in order to create a successful KIE venture. They later move on to jobs in global large firms. The key message is that the different phases call for very diverging managerial skills from the entrepreneurs in order to manage the ambiguous knowledge at hand, and that this is highly affected by identity, image and social relations.

The results of the chapter are related to the development and management phase of the KIE conceptual model (McKelvey and Lassen, 2013), and how resources may be transferred between organizations, and in this case, through individuals and their competencies. This chapter also illustrates how the KIE venture is continuously affected by the traits and personalities of the entrepreneurs, and their ability to translate ambiguous knowledge into tangible opportunities for the venture.

Chapter 9 is entitled 'Knowledge reallocation and challenges for KIE: the case of the European roller coaster industry' and is written by Bram Timmermans, Rudi Bekkers and Luca Bordoli. The case study discusses flows of knowledge within this industry, and especially how existing knowledge can be reallocated and applied in new situations. The mechanisms for doing so may be starting a new venture – either an independent one or one controlled by the parent company – or by a large firm diversifying its existing product portfolio through innovation. The focus is on the influence of pre-entry knowledge on the development of the European roller coaster industry. This chapter provides insights into different modes of entry as well as different characters of pre-entry knowledge. The key message of the chapter is that pre-entry knowledge functions both as a driver of industrial development and as a prerequisite for entry into the industry.

These findings also support the point in the KIE conceptual model (McKelvey and Lassen, 2013) that KIE is a dynamic phenomenon, which spans wider than the context in which the knowledge is originally developed. The results are similar to the results in the chapter by Østergaard and Park, although here the results are extended also into impacts on the large firms' renewal through spin-offs and diversification.

1.3.4 Case Studies in Human Health Care and Food

Human health care and food represent sectors that seem both extremely localized regionally and nationally in terms of delivery of services, on the one hand. On the other hand, these industries are also ones in which there are very strong trends to organize the supply chains and innovation processes globally. They may also be very high tech and quite low tech simultaneously, depending upon where one looks in those supply chains and innovation processes. For example, biotechnology represents a very high-tech and science-based side of health care, whereas provision of basic health care to the poorer segment of the population is usually based upon routines and skilled care providers instead. Human health care and food are also sectors where a large percentage of individual and societal expenditures are made. However, there are problems with rising costs and rising demands for quality. Thus, these sectors also represent areas probably requiring much innovation in the future, in order to solve grand societal challenges like ageing populations and environmental degradation. The old ways of doing things and old ways of organizing knowledge flows and the delivery of products and services will not be sufficient in the future.

The five case studies in Part III on health care and food reflect the diversity of these sectors globally. The chapters discuss a range of issues, relevant for understanding KIE ventures. One set of contributions is related to how cost and price affects innovations and KIE ventures. For example, the chapter on sequencing and bioinformatics in China shows how a KIE venture can reduce costs and still offer very valuable services and products. Another set of contributions has to do with the cost of doing basic science, and the alternative organizational forms and ways of financing further development that the KIE venture may pursue. A final set of contributions relates to networks. The networks are used initially, before the venture is started, but also in later phases of development and management. The networks may be strongly oriented towards scientific and technological knowledge, but many chapters find that a key role of networks is to develop market and business knowledge. Networks also link global large firms to KIE ventures and to universities in low-tech and traditional sectors like food and agriculture.

Chapter 10 is entitled 'How cross-fertilization of high-tech and low-tech sectors creates innovative opportunities: the case of the wearable electrocardiogram' and is written by Alexandra Rosa, Ricardo Mamede and Manuel Mira Godinho. The chapter describes a KIE venture operating in the new area of electronic textiles. The focus is on how the cross-fertilization of different types of knowledge and activity – including academic science, high-tech business and a mature industrial sector – contributes to the development and commercialization of this cross-boundary product. The key message of the chapter is that proximity between scientific and technical organizations with apparently unrelated industrial activities can foster innovation through the integration of their knowledge bases. In this case, it is the proximity and individual interactions between universities, technological centres and hospitals with textiles and clothing that stimulate cross-fertilization.

These findings demonstrate a point also raised in the KIE conceptual model (McKelvey and Lassen, 2013), namely that opportunities for KIE are generated in the combinations of different types of knowledge. The renewal of traditional industries is also very interesting in relation to our claim that KIE occurs throughout the economy. Here, academia has a significant role to play in the development of not only new knowledge, but also the integration of knowledge in commercial solutions in collaboration with firms for more mature industries.

Chapter 11 is entitled 'Building of collaborative network relationships: the case of a corporate spin-off in the medical technology industry' and is written by Jens Laage-Hellman. The chapter describes the founding and development of a corporate spin-off over a period of 20 years. This chapter highlights the importance of different types of collaborations and networks along all stages of the development and management of the venture. All opportunities pursued by the venture are shaped in the interaction with the external ecosystem, including interactions with the parent organization, the academic environment, suppliers and buyers. These longitudinal results form the key message of the chapter, which is that establishing and developing network relationships is a strategically important activity for KIE firms in order to achieve commercial success. The assessment of which network is most valuable may, though, shift over time.

In the KIE conceptual model (McKelvey and Lassen, 2013), the importance of networks is primarily discussed in relation to the development and management of the KIE venture. Networks are also related to accessing resources and ideas during inputs of course. As well illustrated through this chapter, networks also exercise strong influences on KIE in terms of generating and facilitating input, and are an important mechanism for the diffusion of knowledge.

Chapter 12 is entitled 'Collaborative research in innovative food: an example of renewing a traditional low-tech sector' is written by Maureen McKelvey, Daniel Ljungberg and Jens Laage-Hellman. This chapter focuses upon how collaborative research helps develop particularly scientific and technological knowledge for innovative foods. Innovative foods represent one way to develop higher value added products and services in a traditional, highly competitive one like the agriculture and food industries, with trends in recent decades including areas like 'functional foods', 'intelligent foods', 'ecological/green products' and 'nutritionals'. Public policy initiatives for collaborative research between large firms, KIE ventures and universities were designed to stimulate the development of a series of related products, competencies, specific technologies, instruments and measuring techniques. The chapter discusses how primarily the larger firms later develop those ideas into market and business knowledge through new products and services.

In the KIE conceptual model (McKelvey and Lassen, 2013), the focus is largely upon the KIE venture and its relationship to the external environment, including access to resources and ideas. In this chapter, our attention is drawn to the reverse, and how the large firms in traditional industries can also access resources and ideas, for renewal and higher value products and services. In this case, they do so through collaborative research, which involves large firms, public research institutes and universities, as well as occasionally a KIE venture. This chapter demonstrates the importance of renewing not just products or commercialization science but also finding value in other types of technologies, like instruments, measuring techniques to prove the validity of expected benefits and the like.

Chapter 13 is entitled 'Financing and privatizing a visionary research endeavour in proteonomics: the case of ProSci in Australia' and is written by Johan Brink and Maureen McKelvey. This chapter addresses the close linkages between how the firm can use public and private financing to act upon innovative opportunities as well as the complex linkages that founders but also venture capitalists exert upon the later phase of venture management and development. The case study follows an Australian university spin-off venture over a period of 16 years. It illustrates how that venture is continuously shaped and reshaped by the availability of opportunities to finance its research activities, leading it to change organizational form between a research group and a company. The shifting financial milieu not only affects the growth process of the KIE venture, but also shapes the development of knowledge strategies for KIE ventures as a whole. In particular, it affects their ability to finance their visions and the roles and relationship positions of the players in the industry. Over time, the firm and the university act both as competitors, customers and collaborators, due to the changes in financing possibilities. The key message of this chapter is that financing is not only a necessity for the KIE venture to develop, but also shapes the choices made and the opportunities pursued. Hence, the financing strategies have far-reaching consequences for KIE.

In the KIE conceptual model (McKelvey and Lassen, 2013), the importance of financing is discussed as an input variable to KIE, but the model also emphasizes that input is a necessity not only at the early stages of KIE founding, but must be considered at every turn of event. This chapter clearly demonstrates how financing has significant influence on which and how opportunities will be pursued, and the influences on choices of how to manage and develop the venture. This chapter discusses the sometimes complex relationships between investment and performance but also between public knowledge and private knowledge. The academic spin-off was initially a way to keep the research group together, and by the end, the KIE venture was disbanded and the senior researchers moved back to academia.

Chapter 14 is entitled 'Business models in Big Data in China: opportunities through sequencing and bioinformatics' is written by Yanmei Zhu and Maureen McKelvey. This chapter addresses how a KIE venture in China develops its business model and acts upon new global opportunities related to the new technological opportunities afforded by sequencing and bioinformatics, as applied to human health care. What is particularly interesting is why the venture spends so much money to do basic research, and how the same venture moves from focusing on basic research to more private market terms to apply their research results into practical areas and then obtain profit to support their research. This case study is of a Chinese venture, which is outspokenly focused upon a business model organized around 'science and technology push' in areas of genetic sequencing and bioinformatics, although the firm is also affected by the dynamics of basic science and the market. Thus, there may be issues of being active in China, which may be the same or may differ from other parts of the world.

In the KIE conceptual model (McKelvey and Lassen, 2013), the focus is particularly on the KIE venture, but this chapter shows how the entrepreneurial decisions and actions can take different organizational forms, but still follow the same general pattern. In this case, the KIE venture shifts between different organizational forms over time, and this is partly due to demands placed by new opportunities both in scientific research and market prospect.

1.3.5 Further Developing the Ideas

In the final chapter 'Further developing the ideas', we pinpoint and summarize some of the numerous suggestions for further research that have been identified throughout the book. It is our hope that this will inspire the reader to continue his or her studies of the KIE phenomena. The suggestions for further reflections can be used as inspiration for class discussions, Master's thesis projects or academic research projects.

REFERENCE

McKelvey, M. and A.H. Lassen (2013), *Managing Knowledge Intensive Entrepreneurship*, Cheltenham, UK and Northampton, MA, USA: Edward Elgar.

PART I

Transversal technologies, engineering and software

2. How tensions between exploration and exploitation drive the development process of KIE: the case of Sensor Inc.

Astrid Heidemann Lassen

2.1 SETTING THE STAGE

One of the topics often highlighted in both entrepreneurship literature and innovation management literature is related to the difficulties experienced by many knowledge intensive entrepreneurship (KIE) ventures in creating balance between research and development (R&D) activities and activities that focus on bringing products efficiently to market (for example, Lassen and Nielsen, 2009). The difficulties in making a transition from being primarily R&D oriented to being market oriented are found in the fact that, for example, the human resources and the organizational structures and processes that favor research are very different from those required for efficient production. This conflict is what March (1991) referred to as the conflict or tension between exploration and exploitation; both processes are greatly needed, but they have fundamentally different objectives, which require very different mindsets and set-ups.

In particular, in KIE ventures these opposing forces often cause the firm to change once the technology is mature enough and ready for production. Typically supported by venture capital, the transition from R&D facility to production company is a very difficult stage in the KIE venturing process.

In this case study, we describe the development process of a small high-tech venture, which originated as a corporate spin-off company based on a radical rethinking of the technology for carbon dioxide (CO_2) sensing. The case study emphasizes how the tensions between exploration- and exploitation-oriented interests influence the strategic development of a venture. In this sense, the strategic development of the venture is based on dynamic development, flexibility and the ability to design opportunities in step with development. The case study shows how the strategy of the venture post-spin-off gradually develops in step with the maturation process of an organization as well as its technological potential. The overall questions addressed through the case study are:

> How do tensions between exploration and exploitation become visible in the creation process of a KIE venture?
>
> How do such tensions affect the development of the KIE venture?

2.2   THE CASE OF SENSOR INC.

This case study tells the story of the founding and development process of a corporate spin-off company, Sensor Inc. The venture was originally based on a technology project in a large multinational firm, but was spun off into an independent venture.

The creation of this venture was characterized by the high personal involvement of a particularly entrepreneurial individual within the firm; the initial opportunity was recognized by this individual and the development of the opportunity was also largely dependent on his personal efforts to drive the idea forward, rather than on a formal process.

The initial focus at idea creation was a low-cost, low-power, wireless CO_2 sensor, which reduces dependence on infrared source stability by 50 times or more. The idea originated in the area of indoor air quality control, where CO_2 levels are an important variable for air conditioning and for optimization of energy use. However, due to its radical alterations to the techniques for CO_2 sensoring, the new technology also proves highly relevant to a wide range of other areas, such as adaptive oil and gas burner control, liquid/gas ratio control in vaporizers and condensers, multivariate fire detection and control, the food industry (packaging, transportation) and professional farming. Some of these areas lie within the current business interests of the parent company, some are in business areas of tomorrow and some are out of scope and interest.

2.2.1   Opportunity Recognition: Tension between Existing Paradigm and New Idea

The venture was not founded without complications. The idea from the beginning fell between existing business areas of the parent company, meaning that it did not have an obvious home in its initial stage, but could possibly have ended up as either a new business unit or in existing divisions that were prepared to expand their scope. However, as the idea in this case was not clearly aligned with the overall firm strategies, it faced difficulties at all stages and was developed in an atmosphere of ongoing conflict. Although top management personnel consider them-selves entrepreneurial and the parent company claims to have an innova-tive organizational culture, entrepreneurial activity is allowed only within certain predefined limits, and projects that challenge these boundaries are only handled with much difficulty. The inventor, John Smith, remembers the early days of the idea in the following way:

> I was sitting on a bench in Nuremburg when the idea came to me that it should be doable to think about CO_2 sensoring in a completely different way than we normally did. When I came back to the company, I started asking the experts what they thought of my idea. They all said either 'it's not doable' or 'it's so simple that if it was doable, someone would already have thought of it.' As they were the experts on the technology and I just had the idea, it took quite some effort to convince one of the experts to at least try it out, if nothing else then just for the interest of it and to prove me wrong. You can imagine his surprise when the first results came back with positive indications.

The interest created through the first test was sufficient to spark the interest of other experts, and convinced them to follow up on the results. The idea became an informal project, boot-strapping slack resources from official projects to continuously run minor tests and demonstrate the potential of the idea. In this way, the inventor, John Smith, managed to continuously demonstrate features that confirmed the potential for signifi-cant improvements leading to cost reductions, and possible application in a wide cross-section of the firm's products, creating radically new effects in their performance.

After a few years, a breakthrough occurred, and the idea surfaced to become one of the innovative projects with the highest priority within its division. This change happened as top management became increasingly aware of the necessity for more innovative projects with long-term perspectives, and called for such projects from each division. Smith's idea fits perfectly within this strategy and, due to its previous iterate skunk work development, could already show progress on several points, demonstrate patents and quite clearly illustrate its strengths and potential pitfalls. This made for a highly suitable project. Funding was now plentiful, an ad hoc project organization was established, and John Smith was allowed to develop an official project plan that would accommodate the emergent nature of the knowledge and support the continued development of the radical innovation.

As such, we can see that the approach to handling the tensions between the already prevalent knowledge and understanding in the organization and the new idea and the need to rethink existing knowledge is essential to the early development of an idea. The approach includes the ability to work with an idea on the fringes of the formal organization, to use slack resources and to gradually convince the experts who sanction the knowledge and opinions considered relevant for the company. These factors all evolve around the emergent but continuous and goal-oriented design of the innovative opportunity represented by the new technology.

2.2.2 Establishment: Tensions between Internal and External Development

In 2009, Sensor Inc. was officially spun off from the parent company. The inventor, John Smith, who developed the patented ideas behind Sensor Inc., and a colleague, Henry Moseby, were the official founders, together with three investors.

Sensor Inc. now develops infrared optical sensors for measuring environmental and energy parameters, gases, temperatures and so on in harsh environments. The sensors measure temperature and humidity as well as the presence of gases based on patented technology.

The sensors differentiate themselves from others by being able to measure the concentration of gases in extremely harsh environments. Additionally, the Sensor Inc. sensor is capable of measuring several gases simultaneously. Finally, the Sensor Inc. sensor is faster and more durable than other sensors on the market. The main areas of potential application are:

> Horticulture – climate measurement between plants
> Oenology – measurement of grape quality
> Marine – ventilation control and emission measurement.

Of these areas, the main focus is currently on marine emissions. This area of application involves harsh environments, which create very particular circumstances that are highly challenging to existing technologies. The robustness of the Sensor Inc. sensor enables high seas companies to measure emissions inside the exhaust. This in turn allows for more precise engine control, which saves on the resources used. As the costs related to resource expenditure in the marine segment are very high, more precise engine control generates substantial fuel savings and emission reductions. Sensor Inc. has shifted the majority of its attention towards the marine sector in order to develop the strongest value proposition possible.

Of course the decision to establish Sensor Inc. as an independent spin-off company did not come easily. After the parent company was convinced of the potential of the innovative opportunity, it had to weigh the benefits of spinning the venture off, based on a number of different considerations. These included: loss of influence in the direction of the technological development; loss of influence in the areas of application; potential loss of income (from full ownership to minority shareholder); and loss of significant assets in human resources (John Smith and Henry Moseby).

The establishment of Sensor Inc. as an independent venture would also have particular consequences regarding its ability to enter and navigate in the marketplace. Small companies, such as Sensor Inc., are often constrained in negotiations with larger companies. Several of the defined areas of application are dominated by large players, so this was indeed an aspect to consider.

The determining factor in the decision to establish Sensor Inc. as an independent venture was the need to retain focus on the core potential of the innovative opportunity, and to create the best circumstances to fully take advantage of all aspects of the opportunity. Henry Moseby says:

> It is very important that a company focuses on its core activities, and since this sensor product is not a part of the parent company's core business, it was chosen to establish Sensor Inc. as an independent spin-off company ... This setup has created the best conditions for creating growth and progress for the technology, without constantly responding to the strategy and priorities of the parent company.

As for the ability of Sensor Inc. to negotiate with large companies, close ties with the parent company still exist, for example, in terms of the name of the venture, and this provides Sensor Inc. with an image of quality and trustworthiness. This perception often determines access to collaborations with large customers/suppliers. As Henry Moseby expresses it, 'We are able to benefit from advantages from both worlds; we are small and able to move fast, and at the same time we can draw positively on the traditions, experience and name from our mother company.'

As such, it is evident that the resolution of the tension between developing and exploiting the technology internally in the parent company and establishing an independent venture is found in very particular considerations of technology/product features as well as strategic considerations. Central to the successful outcome is that all actors very loyally focus on creating the best possible circumstances for exploring and exploiting the innovative opportunity to the fullest, rather than protecting their individual interests.

2.2.3 Financing Further Development: Tensions between Different Types of Funding

The establishment of Sensor Inc. as an independent venture opened up a number of opportunities, but also created a necessity for the venture to attract sufficient financial resources on their own in order to sustain development and create a viable business.

The company is still highly focused on development and is only gradually turning towards scaling up production. As such, the net sales are still limited and Sensor Inc. is greatly dependent on external investment.

The parent company is still a major investor but not a controlling shareholder. Sensor Inc. is thus truly independent but is still able to draw on the experiences and services of the parent company. As a major investor, the parent company is represented on the board of directors of Sensor Inc. Finally, the parent company has allowed Sensor Inc. to partly retain the name of the mother company.

The financial issues the parent company experienced in 2008 and 2009 caused an unfavorable situation for Sensor Inc., but the venture has been able to overcome this through external investment and funding.

John Smith describes how two kinds of investment money that exists: 'pure investment money' and 'knowledge money.'

Pure investment money is related to business angels who have no real insight into the company and only invest based on an expectation of harvesting high returns on their investment in the short term. While this type of funding is very useful, it also creates pressure to generate substantial turnover within a short time period. While pressures may be positive in the sense that they force the company to focus on the marketplace, they may also have a negative effect as the development phase is necessarily cut shorter, potentially missing essential aspects or opportunities.

Knowledge money, on the other hand, comes with people who also provide benefits to the company; therefore, this type of investor also thinks in longer terms than pure money investors. This type of investor focuses on the development potential of the technology and the company.

Sensor Inc. has been able to attract knowledge money. The external investors have become members of the board of directors, adding additional human resources to Sensor Inc., and bringing their knowledge to the firm.

Besides attracting external investment and venture capital from the parent company, Sensor Inc. has also been able to attract external public funding. Sensor Inc. has been granted 5.2 million euros through public funding. The main contributor is the National Advanced Technology Foundation, which has supported Sensor Inc. through its purpose of enhancing growth and strengthening employment within the fields of research and innovation.

The variety of funding that Sensor Inc. has been able to attract poses a number of opposing demands in terms of focus and return on investment. The public funding demands a focus on exploration of the technological features and possibilities, whereas the funding from the parent company calls for market exploitation. Sensor Inc. has so far been able to balance these opposing demands through careful consideration of the split in shares (and, consequently, the power to impose demands), as well as the obligations connected to different types of venture capital.

2.2.4 Managing the Venture: Tensions between Different Knowledge Bases

When turning to the emerging organizational practices of Sensor Inc. after the venture creation, the issue of opposing knowledge bases becomes apparent. The two founders hold an executive Master of Business Administration (MBA) and a Master in Business Communications, respectively, from different universities. Even though both founders are highly educated and experienced, they hold very different competencies and knowledge bases, and are interested in very different aspects of the venture. Table 2.1 elaborates the titles and characteristics of each founder.

Initially, the inventor, John Smith, appeared to be a natural choice for the position as Chief Executive Officer (CEO) of Sensor Inc.; he had come up with the idea; he had driven the initial development through a resistant organization; and he had developed the arguments as to why Sensor Inc. should be an independent venture.

However, the decision to appoint Henry Moseby as CEO was made by the parent company, which is the main investor. John Smith remembers this in the following way:

> At first it was difficult to let go of the dream of leading my idea the entire way. But of course one person cannot cover all competencies and provide a reasonable result. I knew that in order to create a successful company, we

Table 2.1   Founder characteristics

Name	John Smith	Henry Moseby
Title	Chief Technical Officer	Chief Executive Officer
Degrees	Executive MBA, Master in Management of Technology and BSc in Electrical Engineering	Naval officer, MA in Business Communications
Field of expertise	Business development, innovation, technology research and development and product development	Marketing and communication, network facilitator and business development
Previous experience	John Smith has long experience as a manager in research and development at various international companies and start-ups. For more than 15 years he worked as a manager responsible for a wide range of areas related to technological development and business development. John Smith joined the parent company in 2000	Henry Moseby has long experience within network development as both communications manager and director in different ventures. Most of his experience was acquired within the parent company, which he joined in 2004

needed to assemble a team with a wide range of competencies, and place people in the positions they were best suited for. Looking beyond my personal pride, I knew that Henry was much more market and people oriented than I am. I must admit that I am more interested in the technology than attending-customer meetings. So making Henry the CEO, and me the CTO [Chief Technology Officer], really was the most logical decision. It allowed me to continue focusing on what I do best – developing the technological aspects of the venture. It was extremely challenging and involved much learning from all parts, but it was definitely the right choice.

The balance between the two founders is stable, even though there are many differences between the two, and John Smith describes the success of their collaboration as evidence of the fact that 'We are better at communicating than most people.'

The responsibilities of the two founders are today related to their experience and competencies. John Smith is responsible for the technological aspects of the venture, while Henry Moseby is responsible for more commercial activities, such as network development and sales activities.

This focus is also a result of a very recent change in the management structure spurred by the continuous search to use human resources in the best possible way. As of the beginning of 2012, Henry Moseby has been appointed Chief Communications Officer (CCO) and a new CEO has been brought on board. This decision was in recognition of Henry Moseby's particular competences in market development and sales, as well as the need for a dedicated focus on business and administrative development in broader terms. The new CEO is a former board member of Sensor Inc., has an extensive financial background and has been involved in the growth of several other KIE ventures.

Since it was founded, Sensor Inc. has grown from its staff of two founders into a venture that currently employs 12 full-time employees. In the first years of its existence, the primary focus was on the technological aspects of the venture, giving natural preference to employees with technical expertise. However, in order to prove the business potential of the venture and attract venture capital, it was also necessary for Sensor Inc. to start capitalizing on their products. To facilitate commercial success, the knowledge base now also needs to encompass market-oriented competences.

The past year in particular has brought a lot of changes to the company through fierce development. In relation to the knowledge base the company holds, it faces a challenge to sustain its quality through future growth. With only limited possibilities for employing personnel, striking a balance between the need for knowledge of technological features and the need for market orientation is essential.

John Smith emphasizes that finding the right team does not mean that every employee should be an expert in sensor technology. In fact, he wants the broad focus to be reflected in the composition of employees. To this end, Sensor Inc. has defined specific expectations for its employees: 'The mentality of the employees should be creative, and they should value challenges. The abilities we search for are that they must like to be challenged and they have to challenge others as well.'

The need for opposing types of knowledge is not an insurmountable problem, but it is an issue that demands careful consideration. The limited resources of the venture create a situation where prioritization is necessary, and the wrong decision can have vast consequences. In Sensor

Inc. this challenge is addressed by increasing the focus on the personalities of the potential employees, rather than just their specific technical/ market competences. This is based on a belief that with the right attitude the employees will actually want to participate in activities spanning both technological and market-oriented activities, thereby creating a natural overlap in the knowledge bases. So, where the demands of the development of the technology call for specialists, the human resources (HR) strategy at Sensor Inc. is to look for generalist capabilities to create a balance between the opposing needs of the venture.

At the management level, differences in knowledge are perceived as a strength rather than a weakness, mediated through a strong focus on communication and mutual respect. Additionally, a CEO with a primary focus on business development has been added at the management level, creating a natural interface between the competences and foci of the two founders.

2.2.5 Growing the Venture: Tensions between Technology Development and Market Development

Sensor Inc. has been subject to rapid growth in recent years. From 2009 to 2010 Sensor Inc. increased its gross profit by approximately 116 percent. Likewise, its net worth more than tripled because it was able to attract investors.

The expectations for the future involve continued high growth, which should be facilitated by a product launch in the near future that will bring in revenue. The lack of a product launch is a current barrier that needs to be overcome. John Smith concludes that in order to realize commercial value, products need to be brought to the market. This will also strengthen the attractiveness of Sensor Inc. The market is not considered a hindering factor for this, but issues related to a product launch have been experienced.

> Yes we have developed a sensor technology capable of the most extraordinary things. But in order for our company to be a success, we also continuously need to think about how this technology can be converted into actual products and moved to the market. Sometimes this means taking a lot of steps backwards in order to demonstrate what the technology can and cannot do in the specific context (quality tests). This also means that we often rethink how our organisational set-up should be in order to best take advantage of the technology. This is a real challenge, as the great interest for most of us is to develop the technology. But we have been forced to realise that in order to be attractive for investors and customers these are necessary steps to take every time the technology insights change even the slightest bit. For instance, we

have made changes to our market focus in step with our increased knowledge of the strengths and weaknesses of the technology, as well as where awareness has been raised with customers and investors. The advantages of being as small as we are, is that we are able to make these changes as soon as we become aware of the need to do so. We don't have a lot of resources tied up in only one approach or one system. (Sensor Inc.)

The network relations of Sensor Inc. constitute a major source of influence on the growth of the venture. The relations provide both opportunities and threats. John Smith believes that networks facilitate additional contacts, but it is important to also move past these initial opportunities and close the business deals. This is a capability that Sensor Inc. has had to improve. According to John Smith, 'at some point you need to be a tough negotiator who can close the deals.' Additionally, the networks also pose various possible threats, such as loss of intellectual property and wasted time. At present, the focus is on utilizing the synergies with the business partners to develop the technology to specifically match new areas of application and thereby improve the attractiveness of the company.

As illustrated, the patterns of growth in Sensor Inc. entail a certain discontinuity, swinging between periods of little organizational growth but high focus on technology development, and periods of rapid organizational growth with less focus on technological development. Such discontinuity requires a management approach that can embrace very different requirements in terms of focus, structures, prioritization of tasks, resource allocation, HR demands, training of staff and so on.

2.3   WHAT HAVE WE LEARNED FROM THE CASE OF SENSOR INC.?

Through the case study of Sensor Inc., we have identified various factors related to the tensions experienced by a KIE venture. The tensions have been identified at several different stages of the development of the venture, spanning the very early stages of an idea to the current fast growth of the venture. Additionally, we have demonstrated how such tensions not only pose barriers and challenges for the KIE venture, but also how considerations on how to resolve the tensions actually play a significant role in driving the development of the venture forward. Table 2.2 summarizes the different types of tensions identified and how these affected the development of the KIE venture.

Table 2.2 Tensions in KIE

	Exploration oriented	Exploitation oriented	Effect on the KIE development
Early ideation	New idea, breaking with existing knowledge	Existing paradigm of knowledge	Emergent ideation with high focus on creating proof of concept
Venturing decisions	Independent venture creation	Internal development and application of technology	Focus on how to best explore and exploit all aspects of the innovative opportunity
Financing further development	National Advanced Technology Foundation and university collaboration (long-term perspective on return on investment (ROI))	Corporate venture capital from parent organization (short-term perspective on ROI)	Careful considerations of the obligations and demands attached to different types of venture capital, and matching of these to the vision of the venture
Knowledge bases of the venture	Technological	Market oriented	Hiring based on generalist attitude and personality over specialist knowledge to create natural overlaps between technology and market considerations with limited HR
Expanding the venture	Further research and development	Application in products for the marketplace	Bringing in new CEO to focus on bridging technology versus market development into business development

We argue that the discovery of the effect of tensions is in fact a very significant part of understanding KIE. What we have observed is that very few of the significant events in the development of Sensor Inc. were planned in advance and executed following this plan. Instead, the development was driven by emergent, continuous and proactive considerations of the strategic direction of the venture. This is seen through all the aspects addressed in the case study: the idea, the establishment of the venture, financing, establishing knowledge bases and expanding the venture.

The management group, in particular, emphasizes the need to continuously evaluate and reevaluate, organize and reorganize, in order to be able to both explore and exploit an innovative opportunity in the best possible way. As such, the specifics of the KIE venture emerge as a result of the particular operating circumstances surrounding the enterprise. Here the strategic management becomes primarily an adaptive/reflective process concerned with manipulating a limited amount of resources. The efforts are not concentrated on predicting or controlling the operating environment, but on adapting as quickly as possible to the changing demands of this environment.

2.4 QUESTIONS FOR FURTHER REFLECTION

Discuss the pros and cons of the tensions experienced in KIE ventures.

Which tensions do you foresee in the upcoming years for Sensor Inc., and how would you suggest handling these?

How does the development of KIE ventures differ from the development of internal projects in companies?

REFERENCES

Lassen, A.H. and S.L. Nielsen (2009), 'Corporate entrepreneurship: innovation at the intersection between creative destruction and controlled adaptation', *Journal of Enterprising Culture*, **17** (2), 181–99.
March, J.G. (1991), 'Exploration and exploitation in organisational learning', *Organization Science*, **2** (1), 71–87.

3. Collaborative strategies: how and why academic spin-offs interact with engineering university centers

Maureen McKelvey, Daniel Ljungberg, Olof Zaring, Jens Laage-Hellman and Stefan Szücs

3.1 INTRODUCTION

This chapter addresses knowledge intensive entrepreneurship (KIE) venture development, from the perspective of how and why academic spin-offs engage in collaborative strategies with engineering centers located at the university. The KIE ventures use the centers to access scientific and technological knowledge, as expected, but they are also interested in accessing other resources and networks to help further develop their research, product and market development. Two academic spin-offs are presented, and they have long-term relationships with the engineering faculty, which in this case are European electrical engineering centers.

Collaborative strategies are here studied in terms of how and why the firms are motivated to be involved in university-industry centers, and especially their behavior within these centers in relation to the management and development of the firm. The main foci of interaction appear to be not only the technical research per se but also other aspects like networks and access to students. The main focus is what they do – or do not – get out of this collaboration, after the KIE ventures were formed.

Existing literature on university-industry interactions tends to focus upon large firms (Perkmann and Walsh, 2007; Rothaermel et al., 2007), and provides little guidance about the specific relationship that small KIE firms form with universities and academic scientists. To understand these cases, this chapter therefore provides some more general findings about how and why small KIE firms work with these centers (see Ljungberg and McKelvey, 2012). This broader perspective helps us understand the different ways in which KIE ventures can access resources and ideas, even in later phases, and thereby lays the foundation of the two following specific case studies.

Academic spin-offs are new firms with one or several founders previously or currently employed as university researchers and/or where the venture is (partly) based upon research and technologies developed at a university (Djokovic and Souitaris, 2008; Clarysse et al., 2011). As such, they can be seen as a specific case of KIE, where the sources of KIE are primarily the research environment of the founders' home university. It is generally assumed that the main asset or competitive advantage of academic spin-offs is the technology transferred from a university at foundation, and that this, sometimes called 'resource endowment,' can influence the later development and performance of the KIE venture (for example, Clarysse et al., 2011). This line of thinking has been the main focus in the literature when examining university-industry interaction from the perspective of small firms, in terms of investigating how the specific assumed endowments of these firms (that is, academic research and so on) affect the entrepreneurial ventures' performance (for example, Clarysse et al., 2011; Wennberg et al., 2011). In this way, the existing literature mainly assumes or treats them to be an output of academic research, with scientific development leading to venture creation and commercialization (for a review see, for example, Djokovic and Souitaris, 2008).

This case study examines how these firms continually draw on academia and academic research after their initial foundation phase for managing processes and developing the venture – an area not previously given much attention in the literature. Given their limited resources for assessing and acting upon both technological and market opportunities, networks provide an alternative for more than just scientific and technological knowledge. Collaborative strategies with universities can be a way to overcome such limitations and access knowledge and understanding about technologies, markets and customers. The focus here is upon collaborative strategies for research, product and market development. In both cases, the KIE venture was founded outside the specific research center, so that we provide case studies from foundation onwards in order to distinguish initial sources of resources and ideas (endowments) from collaborative strategies at later phases of venture development.

The first case of a KIE venture gives an example of a long-term relationship between a university and a company, with a particular focus upon what the latter has identified as key network relationships for technological development and commercialization. The second case illustrates the influence and role of the research center on the capture and employment of resources and capabilities of the firm during its market entry, that is, its role in influencing the initial production and delivery of the product to the market.

The chapter addresses the following questions:

> Why and how do KIE ventures engage in collaborative strategies with engineering centers?

> What pre-existing ideas, people and resources (endowments) have influenced the KIE ventures' foundation and development prior to entering a university center?

> What types of collaborative strategies do the KIEs utilize, and what types of benefits do they gain from involvement in a university center?

3.2   CASE STUDIES OF COLLABORATIVE STRATEGIES

This section presents the two case studies of KIE ventures and their collaborative strategies for participating in university-industry research centers. The university-industry research centers studied focus on technical research of relevance for industrial competitiveness within specific fields related to electrical engineering, based upon initiatives from public policy. From the firms' perspectives, these centers represent arenas where different firms and different types of researchers meet to address problems and solutions that arise in applied research. Around one-third of funding has come from the government, one-third from the university and the remaining one-third from participating companies. It is not possible to obtain government funding without matched funding from universities and companies. Given the split funding arrangement, the firms of course access more resources jointly than they would have obtained by their own contributions.

3.2.1   Rationale for KIE Ventures to Interact with Engineering Centers

Engineering centers provide much more than specific problem-solving within science and technology. In order to offer a more general picture and to lay the foundation of the two specific case studies, in this subsection we briefly present the results from a detailed case study of these two engineering centers (see Ljungberg and McKelvey, 2012).

Thus, we address the first question: Why and how do KIE firms engage in collaborative strategies with engineering centers?

Small KIE firms have limited resources, and they primarily participate in the two centers in order to link into academic research, access students, maintain their technical competencies, engage in networks and contacts, interact with large firms and access financial resources (center funding).

While larger firms were primarily interested in participating in the centers to collaborate on and gain fundamental knowledge, which can be developed to innovations within the firms at later stages, small KIE firms were interested in more immediate and applied research and technical problem-solving due to their limited resources. The small firms were also clear that the centers are a cost-efficient way of keeping in touch with the state-of-the-art and to access equipment. As one firm puts it: 'What we get out of [the center] is the luxury to be working with the next generation instruments even though we are a small start-up.' At a low cost, they can find solutions and skilled labor to address their technical problems.

One of the major reported motivations of firms to get involved in the center is to gain access to networks and build up contacts. These networks may be with academic researchers, but may also be networks with other companies, and to stimulate networks outside the boundaries of the center per se. Small KIE ventures were mostly interested in using the centers to develop their business networks, especially in their geographical region. The centers represent a forum to work and interact with large firms and thereby to investigate if the large firms are interested in their specific products and technical solutions. Another aspect of the network was the 'signaling' effect of working with a prominent university and well-known large firms. This gave the small firms more legitimacy.

Networking also seems to play a particular role in the development of knowledge, especially at the individual level. Several firms stated that the centers were useful from a network perspective for accessing competencies and recruiting new employees. In this way, the small KIE firms perceived that participating in the centers made them more visible to students and future employees. Visibility to students, who might otherwise not know about the firm, would enable students to test ideas and work on applied technical problems of potential immediate usefulness for the small firms through MSc and PhD theses but also facilitate their long-term recruitment.

In the following two subsections we present the specific cases of KIE ventures, and their interactions with the research centers. These centers are hosted and located at the same university of technology and administered within the university's electrical engineering department. As such, the centers exist in parallel with the departments and hence the academic researchers do not 'move' completely to the new centers. Instead, the involved senior and tenured researchers remain employed by their department; they allocate a certain percentage of their time to meetings, projects and supervision of involved PhD students within the centers; they interact with companies with regard to project formulation, explaining outcomes and so forth. In contrast, more junior researchers, such as PhD students and postdocs, are more 'dedicated' to a specific project within the center, even if they are also formally employed at a university department.

These centers, acting within two engineering subfields, were started in 1995 and 2007. They have been granted funding for ten years or more, and both have approximately 2.2 million euros in funding annually, including in-kind payment (such as time by firm employees). Both these centers predominantly focus on applied and industrially relevant research within their respective subfield. In one center there are 15 firms involved and in the other nine firms, including small firms. The small KIE ventures participating in the centers are primarily, but not exclusively, academic spin-offs. The participating small firms are, however, not direct spin-offs from these centers, but were founded outside the centers and before their creation.

The cases of KIE ventures working within these engineering university centers address all three questions listed above, and especially the source of KIE and how firm strategy as related to value developed from the collaborative strategies.

3.2.2 Company RayPos

The first case study (RayPos) examines the relationship between a KIE venture and a university-industry center. The venture is an academic spin-off in the medical technology (medtech) industry founded in 2003. At a later stage it became associated with the engineering center.

RayPos is a spin-off from clinical research. The original invention was made by four medical researchers working at university hospitals. The invention, based on many years of clinical research, addresses a key problem in the radiotherapy of cancer patients. To develop the product idea (invention) and transform it into a commercial product, the inventors decided to start their own company. To gain access to the technology needed in order to turn the invention into a practically functioning solution, they made contact with an incubator linked to a major university of technology. This university had a long research tradition in biomedical engineering and had also spun off several medtech companies. After a short period of pre-incubation the four inventors together with the incubator and a recruited Chief Executive Officer (CEO) founded Ray-Pos.

Networks are important to the firm. Its relationships to various external actors constitute the main sources of ideas, knowledge and resources (endowments) that have been brought into the company and shaped its development path. Very early RayPos began to engage part-time consultants. Most of the product development was carried out by these consultants, who had usually been found through the personal networks of the founders. Suppliers also played a decisive role for the early development of the product. For one of the key components in particular it was necessary to find an external production solution. After an intensive search process and four years of discussions and negotiations a fruitful partnership was finally established with one supplier.

Links to the university continue to be made through the medical side, on the one hand. From a networking point of view, the biggest challenge for RayPos was to establish clinical collaborations for the purpose of testing the product and producing evidence about its benefits. Fruitful collaborations have been established with several university clinics – including two places where the inventors are working. The results from the clinical testing will be very important for the company's future marketing. The clinical partners are potential customers. At the same time, they are also the most important partners within the academic sphere.

On the other hand, in terms of technical development, the locating of RayPos close to a university of technology rather than a medical school proved to be advantageous. Thanks to contacts arranged by the incubator, RayPos made contact with two university departments and then later the center.

Access to their engineering and technical knowledge and competencies was crucial for developing the product. Moreover, initially, when the company had only one employee, a large portion of the technical development was carried out by MSc students, mainly in the form of Master's theses. These studies have produced useful knowledge, and the thesis projects have helped the company to make the right technology choices. They presented an opportunity to explore new functionalities, several of which have now been incorporated in the product. RayPos also began to build up its internal organization by recruiting, among others, previous MSc students.

Since this initial relationship, RayPos has continued to have a fruitful exchange with the university of technology. The university-industry center in electrical engineering, as well as departments, is a more recent form of interaction. The firm is one of the industrial partners. It was asked to join, and this was relevant since the center is focusing on technologies of relevance to RayPos, with medicine being one of three selected application areas, and since the firm had informal contacts at the personal level and collaborates through Master's theses projects with the involved departments. The firm had expected to gain access to specialized research equipment, which was quite expensive and necessary for product development, but this did not materialize.

The fact that the center is expected to carry out so-called needs-driven research makes it interesting to RayPos to participate. The firm hopes that its participation will lead to new knowledge that can be used in the company's own product development. 'We would like to have product-oriented projects,' as the CEO puts it.

More concretely, one of the PhD students in the center works on a project involving RayPos and another medtech company. If this study is successful, the results will lead to future improvements of RayPos's product. However, the CEO understands that there is a conflict of interest between the participating companies and the academic researchers, and the practical usefulness of the research result is still uncertain and the firm does not expect that the project will have immediate effects on the company.

One of the experiences of the project in having the PhD student working and physically located in the company's premises is advantageous. This improves the exchange and gives the company an opportunity to acquire new knowledge. It also enables the company to have a real-time impact on the direction of the project.

A second major reason for joining the center, besides the expectations for exploitable research results, is marketing of the company. Participation in the center increases visibility. As a young and very small company RayPos is striving hard to establish itself as a respected player in its business. Being part of the center together with other, larger and better-known companies is expected to have positive effects on the company's image and brand. For example, when the center presents its activities RayPos's project is often mentioned, with the result that the company is taken more seriously.

A third advantage is that the center offers opportunities for networking. RayPos's strategy is to interact as much as possible with various external actors in order to build contacts that may be useful in the future.

Those who stay in the office don't get anything done. One has to be out there and expose oneself to new contact opportunities. That is why we have learnt to know so many people. It is all about contacts, contacts and contacts.

'We do not know with whom we may need to collaborate in the future,' as the CEO puts it. The firm in particular had hoped to establish fruitful interaction with the other partner companies. There are at present two other medtech companies linked to the center. One is a large firm, in which expectations for collaboration have not materialized so far. The other company is a small spin-off from the university's biomedical engineering research. This company is in a similar situation to RayPos, which has enabled the establishment of a fruitful exchange of experiences between the two CEOs. Technical synergies are missing though, since the companies are working with different types of product.

3.2.3 Company Measurement

The second case study examines an academic spin-off called Measurement, and its market entry process during the period 2000–09. This firm also interacted with the engineering center during later phases. The focus here is on public policy measures and the external environment – or what is sometimes called the innovation system. This includes the engineering center, a Science Park and a local government industry support organization (ISO), which support and influence the development of the KIE venture.

Measurement is best defined as an academic spin-off originating with a professor at a department of a university of technology, founded in 2000. By 2012, Measurement was viable in the global market for electromagnetic radiation measurement equipment, where it made its successive entry during 2001–03. The university of technology from which the company was spun off is the same one that also hosts the focal center. The center is active in a technological field closely related to electromagnetic radiation measurement.

Measurement's product is based on an innovation by the professor and can be characterized as belonging to a new product generation in the established market for electromagnetic radiation measurement equipment. The typical customers of the product include wireless device manufacturers, operators and developers as well as universities with relevant research activities. The innovation was brought to market through the creation of the KIE Measurement.

3.2.3.1   Measurement's pre-founding stage

At the pre-founding stage, and especially during the decade prior to entry, the founder worked as part of the scientific community and became a member of a research group at this university. He was thus part of the department that was to become the base for the establishment of the center. He also became active in the commercialization of his own research at this stage, patenting a number of unrelated, scientific discoveries. He successfully proceeded to commercialize those patents, which provided business know-how as well as some funds that were to be used to finance Measurement at a later stage:

> I am a scientist who publishes extensively, but I have also always had a wish to turn all that into something useful to society in the form of a product. This has always been my goal, and since I had successfully commercialized a number of other of my inventions earlier, based on a patent from the 1980s, which has yielded earnings over the years, I knew how this [commercialization] works ... At this stage I was somewhat upset (concerning the prospects of financing a new company) and I saw that the only remaining option was to start a new company, and hire one of my graduate students from the university of technology and to fund this I had to resort to using the incomes from my old patent.

At this pre-founding stage, the university in effect provided the inventor with a low-cost research and development (R&D) capacity: 'We made a substantial part of the research with the help of MSc students and a couple of PhD candidates.'

3.2.3.2   The venture founding stage

Measurement was founded during this stage with the aim of commercializing one of the founder's patents in the market for electromagnetic radiation measurement equipment. The founder was able to provide the necessary capital as well as the required technical expertise, and in addition some commercial know-how. He was also the sole owner, financier and the first CEO of the company.

At this stage the founder, who was also a professor, was also involved as one of the initiators of the center. The center was subsequently formed around the research group at the founder's department at the university and a group of local companies with an interest in certain aspects of electromagnetic radiation technology:

> This is actually one of the places in the world where advanced research is being conducted in this scientific field and one reason for this is of course that we have a locally based company that is a multi-national in this market.

Measurement became one of the corporate members of the center. The company could thereby secure access to a network of local companies in the same industry as well as other actors in the local environment, in particular a science park and a local government ISO. At this stage the science park provided the company with suitable facilities:

> Measurement needed expanded and adapted facilities, and the science park had some free space so we got offices and labs adjacent to where the production takes place and this simplified matters for us.

Measurement then made a first attempt to enter the market at this stage under the management of the founder/CEO but it was found to be lacking management and market expertise, and the attempt did not lead to any sales. The founder was provided with a timely opportunity to change.

3.2.3.3 Measurement's market entry stage

During market entry stage Measurement utilized its newly acquired network in local industry to successfully hire a new CEO from one of the leading local companies in the industry.

> I am a scientist, my principal networks are within the research community, this means that I don't know of people capable of managing a business, but I got lucky finally. I heard of a highly capable person from this multinational wireless company (a member of the center), who used to be a manager there but was in the process of leaving that company, and who was actually working at the science park on behalf of his employer.

The new CEO's task was to effectuate the second attempt of market entry for the company. To this end the company was able to make further use of the networks and contacts it had obtained as part of the center, to the local industry and other actors. Moreover, the government ISO was able to provide low-cost access to the global market for electromagnetic radiation measurement equipment through its sponsorship of participation in industry fairs worldwide. The founder: 'I have to mention that the ISO has been incredibly important in providing market channels for us, it could only have been possible with their help.'

During this market entry stage Measurement also continued to improve its reputation and make use of low-cost labor for its now intensive R&D work in the form of postgraduate students.

> Thus, Measurement has obtained legitimacy from participating in the center, and we have thereby received financing to run a pilot project, which will develop into a full project all about our measurement technology, and all in all this means that 3 people work for us using center funding.

These were accessed primarily through the university and partly financed by the center. This stage ended with the successful delivery of the company's first product to a customer.

During the latter part of the commercialization process important resources and capabilities were provided and channeled through the center, and these gave Measurement access to new local actors, such as the science park and the ISO run by the regional government. Participation further gave the company legitimacy in relation to a local industry network, which supported the appropriation of commercial capabilities. This gave Measurement management and market expertise, as well as access to cost-effective marketing channels.

3.3 WHAT HAVE WE LEARNED?

The three questions posed at the beginning of this chapter are:

> Why and how do KIE ventures engage in collaborative strategies with engineering centers?

> What pre-existing ideas, people and resources (endowments) have influenced the KIE ventures' foundation and development, prior to entering a university center?

> What types of collaborative strategies do the KIEs utilize, and what types of benefits do they gain from the involvement in a university center?

With regard to the first question, we have seen that small KIE ventures overall engage in engineering centers to access resources, such as competencies and recruitment, state-of-the-art equipment and cheap labor (such as MSc students) that due to their small size and limited resources are scarce and hard to come by. They also engage in collaborative research strategies to access networks, especially to gain contacts with large firms, for collaboration and marketing purposes. This can be summarized as:

(a) Interaction with universities is not only, or primarily, about getting new product ideas. More importantly, companies get a chance to access research-based knowledge and competencies that can be transferred to the company and used in internal product development.

(b) Advanced education including MSc and PhD students, through theses and other educational projects, constitute a vital resource for this technology transfer.

(c) Besides knowledge and competencies, companies can benefit from university relationships by gaining access to advanced scientific instruments. This is of particular importance to young start-ups, which normally cannot afford to buy such equipment.

(d) Contacts with a particular research center may be part of a broader and long-term interface with the university – where the company also has contacts with other units and in other forms. In this context, the center activities can be a valuable catalyser of other joint activities between the company and the university.

(e) For a company, participation in a research center is not only about collaboration with the academic researchers. The opportunity to interact and build relationships with other firms is also valued.

With regard to the second and third questions, we can see that the two cases of KIE ventures show both similarities and differences in terms of collaborative strategies, and that the combined picture from these two cases is in line with the general findings of KIE ventures' engagement in these centers.

When it comes to the sources of KIE, that is, endowments, in these two cases, we see that, in line with both being academic spin-offs, the university system in general has played an important part in supporting and facilitating technology development before foundation and during early phases of venture development. In the RayPos case, the original idea was identified by the company founders in their positions as medical researchers. Moreover, the development was importantly facilitated by the firm being connected to an incubator, which arranged contacts with university departments that initially provided crucial aid in technology development, not least in terms of MSc students. In the second case, Measurement was provided with crucial endowments, prior to the company being founded, in the form of patents held by the founder based on inventions made during his research as an employed university researcher. The university also provided qualified low-cost labor that supported the development of the innovations prior to the foundation of the firm.

When we turn to the motivations of the two firms to engage in the centers and the benefits they gain from this, that is, their collaborative strategies, we see that interaction for technology development seems to be less important at these later phases of venture development. This is especially apparent in the first case, in which RayPos hopes that its participation will lead to future improvements of its product, but perceives that the practical usefulness of the research and the immediate effects on the company is still uncertain. However, the firms acknowledge that participating in the centers provides them with low-cost R&D labor, in terms of MSc and PhD students, which seems to have been especially important in the second case.

The main advantages for these two KIE ventures to be involved in the centers seems to be to accessing networks, especially in terms of gaining contacts with other firms. However, the rationale and outcomes for networking within the center differ between the two cases. In the first case, RayPos has mainly used the center for accessing networks for marketing and legitimacy as well as for finding potential collaborators in terms of contacts with other firms. In the second case, Measurement is also largely a case about networking, but rather in terms of utilizing the contacts made from the center to the local industry and other actors to gain and recruit managerial competencies to facilitate market entry.

There are some important differences between the two cases. In the case of RayPos, none of the inventors/founders came from the center (or university of technology). The center has played a relatively limited role for the company, and instead represents one of many ways to interact with universities. In the case of Measurement, the founder is a professor and working for the center, and the center plays an important role for the company, both for technical knowledge and accessing market knowledge through networks with large companies and other local actors.

3.4   QUESTIONS FOR FURTHER REFLECTION

What is the rationale, from the perspective of the firm, for understanding why your academic spin-offs should engage in collaborative strategies with engineering centers?

Given what you have learned about these cases, would you recommend that an academic spin-off should interact with a university center located close geographically but of lower research quality or a university center located in another country but of the highest international research quality?

How can public policy facilitate academic spin-offs to interact with universities?

REFERENCES

Clarysse, B., M. Wright and E. van de Velde (2011), 'Entrepreneurial origin, technological knowledge, and the growth of spin-off companies', *Journal of Management Studies*, **48**, 1420–42.

Djokovic, D. and V. Souitaris (2008), 'Spinouts from academic institutions: a literature review with suggestions for further research', *Journal of Technology Transfer*, **33**, 225–47.

Ljungberg, D. and M. McKelvey (2012), *Collaboration Strategies in University-Industry Relationships*, Deliverable No. 1.8.3, AEGIS, 7th Framework Programme for Research and Technological Development.

Perkmann, M. and K. Walsh (2007), 'University-industry relationships and open innovation: towards a research agenda', *International Journal of Management Reviews*, **9**, 259–80.

Rothaermel, F.T., S.D. Agung and L. Jiang (2007), 'University entrepreneurship: a taxonomy of the literature', *Industrial and Corporate Change*, **16**, 691–791.

Wennberg, K., J. Wiklund and M. Wright (2011), 'The effectiveness of university knowledge spillovers: performance differences between university spinoffs and corporate spinoffs', *Research Policy*, **40**, 1128–43.

4. Interaction as a strategy in knowledge intensive entrepreneurship: the case of an ERP software company

Olof Zaring

4.1 INTRODUCTION

This case study is about the development process of a new entrepreneurial venture, the software company IJK, seen over a prolonged period. The case study follows the company during the 1983–2003 period. IJK went through three distinct phases during this time span when it pursued different entrepreneurial strategies.

The case study covers the successful management of expansion and consolidation in the software industry and shows how this can be a prolonged process, where a company develops products, expands its market reach and faces crisis. The case especially covers the relationship between expansion strategies, financing and ownership, and product development and illustrates the use of partnerships as a management tool in a knowledge intensive enterprise.

The case study illustrates how enterprise growth is not a particularly predictable process to the entrepreneur. Managing growth in an entrepreneurial enterprise is as much about balancing ups and downs due to uncertainty in market conditions, technology and the supply of risk capital as well as about alleviating tensions between entrepreneurial ambition and practicality. In particular the case study serves as a contrast to a basic 'textbook case' of entrepreneurship where linear business planning is the tool of choice and where expansion goes according to the original planning, which is not the focus in this book. Rather we illustrate here that entrepreneurship is often a non-linear process that defies planning efforts:

- It is not sufficient to make a business plan with a specific strategy for expansion and expect that it will hold for any length of time.
- It is easy to underestimate the continuous need for risk capital during the expansion of an entrepreneurial enterprise; capital is needed for many purposes in addition to research and development (R&D).
- Market conditions, technology and the supply of risk capital interact and the result may be a cyclical development pattern for an enterprise.

The following questions, in relation to the case study in this chapter, might be of interest to students of knowledge intensive entrepreneurship (KIE):

How does this company change its focus over time?

How does it deal with growth and contraction?

How is the company affected by the interactions between the product and services they offer, the financing and their partnerships?

How does a venture deal with crises such as the burst of the information technology (IT) bubble in 2000? How does this affect their business?

4.2 CASE DESCRIPTION

IJK was founded in 1983 by a group of engineering students still living in a hostel. They were the original entrepreneurs and remained as major owners and top managers in the company for a period of 20 years. Originally the company provided software consultancy services, particularly in relational database technology. The company entered the market as a software consultancy firm to the energy utilities industry, and particularly for maintenance systems. IJK subsequently launched its first integrated software product in 1990: a software system for Enterprise Resource Planning (ERP).[1] The company has been active in this market since that point in time and remains a global supplier of ERP systems. Today IJK develops and supplies ERP systems to medium-sized and large enterprises in a broad range of industries, globally. Thus IJK was, and remains, an actor in the same market segment as ERP system providers SAP and Oracle. IJK still delivers consultancy services but they are now directly related to the installation and use of the offered software system, known as 'System6'. IJK receives earnings from three main sources: software license fees, software consultancy and systems support contracts to customers.

IJK grew extensively during the late 1990s as a consequence of a pronounced growth strategy to reach this market position. At that time IJK became the fifth company in size in its global market segment. The growth strategy eventually resulted in negative results and cash flows as the market for ERP systems weakened around the year 2000. The company shifted its strategic focus and tried to balance cost reductions with continued growth through partnerships with other software companies.

The founders of IJK remained the major owners, and the structure of ownership did not change significantly until a well-known European investor entered as an owner in 2000 during the company's crisis. This investor continued to invest in IJK and became its largest owner by 2003. The company to a large extent financed its expansion with issues of shares to the stock market and the number of outstanding shares increased threefold during the 1998–2003 period.

The following case description is divided into three phases: (1) Pre 1995: focusing the enterprise; (2) 1995–99: upswing, expansion; and (3) 2000–03: downswing, adaptation.

4.2.1 Pre 1995: Focusing the Enterprise

In 1983 the IJK software company was started by five engineering students at a technical university. The university was located in a city that was incidentally the home to the national aerospace industry and also to IJK's two main domestic competitors. During its first years the company was financed internally and through bank lending. Only when the company established its international subsidiary in Poland in 1991 did it begin to raise capital from investors.

In 1983 the offering consisted solely of software related services. The main services then provided were:

- software services, such as systems development
- technical and economic documentation services for software systems
- project management services for implementing software solutions to management problems.

During its first years of operations in the 1980s IJK accumulated specific expertise in relational database technology and linked this to knowledge on the management of preventive maintenance, which it acquired in connection with assignments in the nuclear power industry. This resulted in the development of 'IJK Maintenance,' the first software product of IJK, which was launched in 1986.

In 1985 IJK decided to diversify further, and acquired two other IT companies and changed the product offering to also include an in-house manufacturing capacity for computer hardware. The major customer then was Nokia, at the time in the process of developing the 'Luxor' personal computer with IJK as a hardware supplier. During 1986 Nokia decided to terminate the development work on Luxor computers. This hit one division of IJK especially hard since its operations were to a large extent based on the Luxor computer. This turn of events forced IJK into its first restructuring of the company. This resulted in a narrower strategic focus with two business areas in 1987, banking and finance and industrial manufacturing, each aimed at a specific customer category for IJK's software related products.

Operations not associated with these areas were liquidated. The strategic focus on the two business areas, and with increased recruitment and investments in product development, resulted in a stronger market position during the following years. IJK continued to expand in 1988. Net sales increased from 3.0 to 3.7 million euros, the number of employees rose from 32 to 43. IJK also launched three new software modules: an accounting module, a production management module and a reporting module. The new modules now meant that IJK had a complete Oracle[2]-based solution for industrial manufacturing companies in 1988. During 1989 and 1990 IJK incorporated the modules into one integrated platform called 'System5.' The modules of this platform were eventually converted to relational database technology, which transformed 'System5' into one of the most modern systems in its market at the time. Once IJK began offering an integrated product it invested heavily in R&D. The R&D spending increased rapidly with the decision made to convert 'System5' to 'System6' in 1994. The ratio between R&D spending and net sales has, however, been rather stable between 18 to 21 percent during all phases described in this case study.

'System5' was further developed during 1991 and 1992. In 1992 IJK used a newly established development organization for System5 in an international environment to this end. This is the first time IJK declared any international ambitions, which were emphasized through the estab-lishment of a subsidiary in Poland.

4.2.1.1 First phase summary

As explained in the introduction, the cases cover three phases. During the first phase 1983–94, described in this section, the company originally had a diversified product offering that did not succeed. IJK then proceeded to narrow its product focus and managed to obtain capital to finance the necessary R&D to develop and maintain a viable integrated software product, known as 'System5' at the end of the first phase.

4.2.2   1995–99: Upswing, Expansion

4.2.2.1   Strategic orientation
During the second half of the 1990s IJK invested heavily in a new international growth strategy, primarily a geographical expansion one. IJK was also the fastest growing supplier of ERP systems during the years 1997–99, globally. The company's net sales rose from 24 million euros in 1995 to 315 million euros in 2001. At the end of 2000 IJK had a presence in 43 countries.

IJK pursued this expansion primarily through acquisitions and partnerships with established software companies in each targeted international market, especially in the USA. Several issues of new shares were made in order to finance the expansion. This was accomplished by IJK acquiring software developers and suppliers of business applications, incorporating parts of their software as new features in 'System5' and 'System6.' Another part of the strategy was to thereby also acquire access to the existing customer base of those companies as well as local market and language knowledge. The average number of employees increased dramatically during the years 1997–2000 (Figure 4.1). Not surprisingly, this coincides with IJK's strong growth policy. IJK also invested heavily in R&D during this phase. The cost of R&D increased from 12 million euros in 1997 to 55 million euros in 2001.

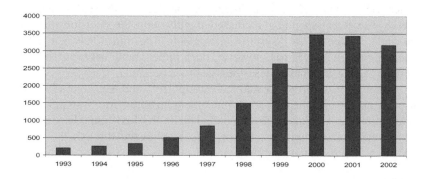

Figure 4.1   The average number of employees in IJK between 1993 and 2002

While most competitors pursued a strategy where consultancy was an integral part of their offering, IJK followed another path. Beginning in the USA, IJK partnered with companies that would sell System6 and provide the services themselves. This was originally due to the difficulty in terms of cost and time for a small European company in entering the US market experienced by IJK. Another reason was to avoid problems and competition with local partners when IJK should have their own consultancy operation in a country. It also proved to be a way of quickly expanding internationally to a relatively low cost. This strategy meant less revenue from services compared with competitors. On the other hand, it meant that more software licenses were sold to customers resulting in future support fees being generated.

4.2.2.2 Product and services
In 1994 IJK began the project to transfer 'System4' to an object-oriented technology. The object-oriented technology enabled IJK to construct near tailor made solutions by different combinations of objects or modules to suit the individual customer. It also enabled IJK to provide special combinations of modules in systems tailored for specific industries. The following years were spent developing the system, and new features such as support for mobile phones, were added. 'System6' was launched in 1997 entirely programmed in object-oriented technology. In the same year IJK launched web clients for 'System6.' IJK has launched a new version of 'System6' annually since 1997, adding incremental improvements, new modules, improved usability and functionality and widened compatibility.

IJK also began to allow the integration of System6 in other vendors' systems: IJK aimed at becoming a specialized supplier also to other actors in the software industry, who then sells and installs to end customers. This model is radically different from selling and implementing ERP systems directly to end customers.

4.2.2.3 Market developments
The market for ERP systems grew rapidly between 1995 and 1998. During 1998 the rate of market growth decreased and continued to decline during 1999. The lowered growth was believed to be caused by companies focusing their IT resources on the Y2K problem rather than on investing in new systems.

4.2.2.4 Financing the expansion
In 1996 IJK issued shares to 12 European institutions. This was IJK's first issue of shares and the new capital was needed to finance the

introduction of IJK's products abroad, primarily in Western Europe, Asia and the USA. It was also the first step towards IJK entering the stock market. Prior to this stock issue IJK was entirely owned by its managers and employees. The issue of shares generated 12.5 million euros, and in the annual report for 1996 IJK announced its intention to enter the Stockholm Stock Exchange within the first six months of 1997. At the same time they would make a new issue of shares worth 25 million euros.

However, IJK did not then manage to meet the requirements of the Stock Exchange. IJK's low profitability, high R&D costs and the fact that IJK entry on the international market was behind its major competitors were the reasons for the Stock Exchange denying IJK stock market entry. Early in 1998 IJK again announced their intention to enter the stock market the same year and managed to do so in that year. In the ensuing years a series of issues of shares raised a total of 200 million euros.

4.2.2.5   Second phase summary
The second phase, 1995–99, was characterized by the company pursuing a quite successful global expansion strategy. The strategy was to prioritize growth over profitability in order to attain economics of scale and market penetration, as explained below. The strategy included the use of alliances with other software companies as a way of supporting the expansion.

4.2.3   2000–03: Downswing, Adaptation

IJK went through many changes in the 2000–03 period; these changes were driven by difficulties in maintaining profitability and growth caused by the burst of the stock market bubble in the year 2000, which affected end customers' willingness to invest in ERP systems. The stock market crisis hit the IT industry in early 2001 and this was the major reason for IJK's and the software industry's difficulties at that time. Even though IJK managed to maintain its market share, profitability plummeted and the company reported a large financial loss for that year. The stock market crash prevented the company from raising more capital and as the company's organization was poised for continuous growth, it proved over-dimensioned for a situation of negative growth in the market. The pronounced growth strategy officially decreased in pace in December 2000 when the board of directors decided to strengthen the company's financial position. The intention was to give priority to generating an increased cash flow and increase profitability and attempt to maintain growth and R&D spending. The future expansion was to be conducted from a more stable financial position. The specific target was to lower costs by 20 million euros during 2001. The result was a 34 million euros cost reduction by the end of that year. The cost reductions continued during 2002 with 30 million euros and an additional 30 million SEK for 2003.

During 2001 IJK further emphasized its strategy with regard to creating new alliances and partnerships. Contrary to many of its competitors, IJK expected that partners increasingly would manage marketing, sales and implementation. IJK had partners that managed implementation and installation of the 'System6' ERP software, but needed additional ones to further increase sales. In the beginning of 2001 partners accounted for 10 percent of the sales. Another reason for IJK establishing alliances and partnerships was to strengthen their capacity for handling large multinational customers (Table 4.1).

Table 4.1   Summary of major partnerships and acquisitions

Year	Partner (P)/Acquisition (A)	Region	Purpose
1995	Versa Torron Sistekindo (P)	Asia	Marketing and distribution
1996	Avalon (A)	USA	Access to customers and market
1997	Pro:Con (A)	Nordic	Made IJK the largest supplier in Denmark. Also strengthened IJK's competence within materials and production management
1997	SoftWind (A)	Nordic	Access to SoftWind's large cutsomers (Astra, ABB and others). Similar technology
1997	Eurinfo SA (A)	Europe	Software development company
1997	Methodus Ltda (A)	Latin America	Distributor
1997	Cognos (P)	USA	Product development
1997	Hyundai (P)	Asia	Market access, marketing and distribution
1998	Industridokumentation AB (IDOK) (A)	Nordic	Complementary technology in engineering and documentation management. Access to IDOK's large customer base
1998	Iqsoft (A)	Europe	

Year	Partner (P)/Acquisition (A)	Region	Purpose
1998	GSB Gmbh (A)	Europe	Access to customers in Europe and technology integration in human resources management
1998	Menthor Technologies (A)	Latin America	
1998	Microsoft (P)	USA	Product development
1998	Hewlett-Packard (P)	Nordic	Credibility
1998	Prolog (P)	Latin America	Distributor
1998	Applied Micro (P)	USA	Marketing and installation
1998	Texas Daltech (P)	USA	Marketing
1999	Exactium (A)	Israel and USA	Access to US market and technology integration in sales support
1999	Brainware (A)	Europe	Distributor
1999	Effective Mangement Systems (EMS) (A)	USA	Access to customers and market
1999	Strategic Information Group (SIG) (P)	USA	Marketing and implementation
1999	American Express Tax and Business Services (P)	USA	Marketing and sales
1999	Siemens (P)	Europe	Marketing
2000	Vendimo Business Solutions AB (Diamo AB) (A)	Nordic	Complementary technology within sales support systems
2000	IM Brännwall AB (A)	Nordic	
2000	Elanor (A)	Europe	Access to customers and market
2000	BBC Consulting Group (A)	USA	Expertise in Internet-based business-to-business solutions and market access
2000	Parade Software Pty, Ltd (A)	Australia	Marketing and distribution
2000	ABB Automation (P)	Global?	Integration in ABB's offering, i.e. distribution
2000	Atos Origin (P)	Europe and USA	Marketing, sales and implementation

Year	Partner (P)/Acquisition (A)	Region	Purpose
2000	BAE Systems (P)	Global?	Joint venture to target civil aviation and defense industries
2000	Cap Gemini Ernst & Young (P)	Global	Joint offering
2000	IBM (P)	US?	Joint sales initiatives and product development
2000	Nec (P)	Global	Joint offering and product development in Internet-based business applications
2000	Roxen Internet Software (P)	USA	Product development
2000	Alfaskop (P)	Nordic	Product development
2000	Softlab (P)	Europe	Product development
2000	Exodus Communication (P)	Europe	Product development
2000	Metrix (P)		Joint offering of integrated solutions for customer relationship management (CRM) and e-business
2000	Knosys (P)	USA	Product development
2001	ABB (P)	Global?	Joint offering of completely integrated remote system for optimization of production and maintenance management
2001	Telia (P)	Nordic	Product development
2001	Nihon Unisys (P)	Asia	Product development
2001	Manpower (P)	Nordic	Joint venture in human resources management
2001	Atos Origin (P)	Europe and USA	Expanded partnership
2001	Streamserve (P)	Nordic	Product development
2001	Pipechain (P)	Nordic	Product development
2001	Indigo (P)	Japan	Product development
2001	Kommentus (P)	Nordic	Joint effort to target public sector
2001	Readsoft (P)	Nordic	Product development
2001	IBM (P) (P)	Global	Expanded partnership

Year	Partner (P)/Acquisition (A)	Region	Purpose
2001	GE Engine Services (P)	Global	Jointly market IJK Aviation software to the commercial aviation maintenance repair and overhaul (MRO) industry
2002	DNV Software (P)	Nordic	Product development aimed at offshore industry
2002	Intentia (P)	Nordic	Joint effort to analyse interaction between value chains
2002	Northrop Grumman	USA	Marketing to defense industry
2002	Sun Microsystems	USA	Product development and marketing

Thus, in 2001 IJK started to reduce costs in a program to achieve balance in the company's finances. Up until that point in time IJK had mostly been able to balance its costs through increased revenues from the growth in company sales resulting from the growth strategy. As the market weakened the revenues no longer increased at the necessary pace. IJK therefore started to reduce operating costs with the aim to reach profitability during 2001. The decision to slow the expansion was received very positively by the stock market – the share price for IJK stock increased by 61 percent. The general opinion was that IJK had grown too much too fast. IJK also received a loan of 20 million euros from a consortium consisting of major owners.

The aim for the cost reduction program was to reduce the workforce by 260 people and reduce costs by 20 million euros in 2001. IJK started by reducing the consultancy personnel in Europe. Reduction of personnel in the USA followed later in that year. The program had been implemented in mid-2001 and IJK showed a promising positive result for the second quarter of 2001 at two million euros. However, the crisis worsened and the cost reduction program proved insufficient. The financial result was –11.6 million euros for the last quarter and –37.6 million euros for 2001.

The cost reduction program was not the only major change in 2001. Michael Hamilton entered as the major owner at the end of 2000 and was appointed chairman of the board in January 2001. He then continuously increased his ownership share in the company. In March 2003 he owned 36.7 percent of the votes and 41.3 percent of the capital of IJK.

IJK continued to try to balance the reduction of costs with expansion during 2002. The company closed offices and reduced personnel. At the same time they continued to partner with software companies that would market, sell and install their products. IJK continued having difficulties with their cash flow despite the initiatives taken to reduce costs. The main reason was probably the weak market at the time. Many prospective customers had a wait-and-see attitude towards acquiring ERP systems. This not only weakened demand but also made the market very difficult to predict. This resulted in a financial result of −76 million euros in 2002. The share price dropped 16 percent as a result.

The weak financial result in 2002 forced IJK to further cost reductions in 2003. In the beginning of 2003 IJK cut personnel by an additional 350 people, primarily within product development. The owners also extended a new loan of 21.5 million euros. This meant that in the 1997–2007 period IJK received a total of 220 million euros from its owners. At the same time a new managing director was appointed. At this point the company's financial situation stabilized and it showed positive financial results for 2004.

4.2.3.1 Third phase summary

In the third phase, 2000–03, IJK was hit with a crisis that was spurred by the burst of the stock market bubble in 2000. The company responded by cutting costs while trying to maintain its global expansion strategy. However, this proved costly to the original owners. Augusto Lolito, long-time managing director, had to relinquish control. Up until 2002 he had been one of the original entrepreneurs, the main owner, chairman of the board and the managing director. The new dominant owner Michael Hamilton replaced Augusto Lolito as chairman of the board in 2001, and in early 2003 a new managing director was appointed.

4.3 WHAT HAVE WE LEARNED?

In the introduction to the case study four questions were posed. In this section we provide some answers to the questions, and also analyse the case to arrive at our main conclusions.

1. How does this company change its focus over time? The company changed focus in an interplay with strategic intention and crisis. By this we refer to the fact that the company changed its focus when it became obvious that the original knowledge intensive entreprenuerial strategy did not work and that the company's existence was

threatened by pursuing it further. A good example is when IJK is forced to narrow its originally broader focus in the first phase, when a major customer left the company.

2.   How does it deal with growth and contraction? Although being a knowledge intensive enterprise the company was not insulated from business realities. The company dealt with growth by raising capital to finance growth as can be expected, but IJK also speeded the growth through the use of alliances, a less costly way to reach customers. The company responded to market contraction by rather standard cost-cutting measures, which proved sufficient and successful.

3.   How is the venture affected by the interactions between the product and services they offer, the financing and their partnerships? IJK's approach to this evolved over time into a reliance of partnerships to both reach a wider market, to reduce the cost of acquiring customers as well as a way of acquiring necessary new knowledge to develop its product offering. This reduced the need to finance market expansion, and the capital the company did raise could be used for internal R&D to a larger extent. One could say that the company enhanced the knowledge content of its product in this way. This most likely made the product offering more competitive. Once the company moved from a diversified product offering in the first phase it used the same approach in the next two phases. Even the crisis of the third phase did not fundamentally change the company's approach in the product offering or how its product was developed, or how to reach its customers.

4.   How does a venture deal with crises such as the burst of the IT bubble in 2000? How does this affect their business? In this case the company dealt with crisis by managing to cut costs while maintaining the confidence of its owners to such a degree that they supplied additional capital to bridge the crisis. This took place at the cost of the original owners finally losing control of the company.

One way of managing growth in an entrepreneurial enterprise such as IJK is that it is of major importance to find a model where uncertainty in market conditions, costs of R&D technology and the supply of risk capital can be managed by finding an arrangement with partners who are willing to take on certain costs and responsibilities. In particular the IJK case shows that KIE using business planning might be difficult because the growth of such a venture might well follow a non-linear process that defies original planning efforts. Flexibility within the management team is a most important trait in a knowledge intensive enterprise because:

- A business plan for expansion should not be expected to hold for any length of time.
- It is easy to underestimate the continuous need for risk capital during the expansion of an entrepreneurial enterprise.
- Market conditions, technology and the supply of risk capital interact and the result may be a cyclical, unpredictable development pattern for an enterprise.

To understand KIE, students (and managers) need to have a wide repertoire of management skills in addition to any venture-specific expertise. The case study shows that the successful management of expansion and consolidation in KIE may be a prolonged process requiring financial as well as management stamina, where a company develops products, expands its market reach and faces crisis. Students need to pay special attention to potential interactions between strategy, finance, R&D and the use of partnerships as a management tool to reduce risk capital needs in a knowledge intensive enterprise.

4.4 QUESTION FOR FURTHER REFLECTION

IJK's partnerships and alliances are described in Table 4.1. Is there a pattern in how they develop over time?

NOTES

1. ERP systems integrate management information across all functions, for example, manufacturing, accounting and marketing, within an organization in a software application that is meant to facilitate the flow of information between all parts of a business.
2. A de facto technological standard for relational databases at this time.

5. Managing international expansion in a KIE venture: going global in Alpha Composites

Dmitrij Slepniov and Brian Vejrum Waehrens

5.1 INTRODUCTION

In 2009, Alpha Composites, a small innovative European company specializing in glass fibre composite materials, announced a start-up of a new production unit in China. This was a big decision for Alpha's Chief Executive Officer (CEO), whose parents had established the company together 30 years earlier. Despite having sales internationally almost from the inception of the venture, Alpha developed, produced and supplied composite profiles only from their home base in Europe. Now, all of that was about to change as the company was entering a new stage in its international development by changing its operations configuration and establishing its base in China.

On the one hand, the decision seemed like a no-brainer. While many other countries fell into an economic coma after the recession struck in 2008, China continued to grow at a double-digit rate, proving the country's potential to be the world's growth engine in terms of output and consumption. On the other hand, the business environment in developing countries, China among them, was still very demanding, both in terms of market entry and day-to-day management. Many CEOs of Western companies were losing sleep over partners' predatory behaviour, competition from cut-price copycats of their own products and bewildering and arbitrary legislation.

Dealing with these caveats would be difficult even for large companies that had operated internationally for decades. Alpha had not. Moreover, as a small- and medium-sized enterprise (SME), it had rather scarce managerial resources for developing and implementing an effective strategy for the start-up in China, arguably the world's most complicated and competitive market. However, the founders and the CEO firmly believed that if Alpha did not try to establish a new venture in an international setting, it would be pushed aside by rivals, old and new, that were already using fast-developing emerging countries to transform their competitive positions.

There were other important factors that Alpha had to consider in its global move – the company's values, unique knowledge and technology that over the years had helped the company to develop its innovative profile and become one of Europe's leading providers of pioneering composite profiles solutions. To a large extent, these strategic assets were a result of extensive investments the company had made into its engineering organization, as well as long-term collaboration with its customers and more than 20 research centres and universities from all over Europe. If managed appropriately, Alpha's strategic assets could become one of the most important determinants of success and competitive advantage in its international expansion. As examples of many other companies show, that's often easier said than done.

Alpha's case, presented in the next section, describes an international expansion journey and its underlying dynamics. The case study highlights how the operations configuration and the relationships between key players do not stay constant over time. Rather, they shift and adapt to internal and external stimuli. The case study explores these stimuli in retrospect and describes how the company attempted to reconcile changing requirements with its knowledge resources and capabilities. By exploring Alpha's production start-up in China, this case study sets out to uncover how to manage development and international expansion in knowledge intensive entrepreneurship (KIE) ventures, including issues related to knowledge intensity and new products and services. The case study can support discussions related to international expansion and development of KIE ventures (especially in emerging markets). The case study focuses on the following interrelated questions:

Why and how does a KIE venture apply its knowledge resources globally?

What are the main factors and determinants of such an application?

5.2 THE CASE OF ALPHA COMPOSITES

5.2.1 How it All Began

Alpha's history began in 1979 when two entrepreneurs, husband and wife, established their venture that would specialize in composite materials development and production. The family ownership of the business continues today, with one of the founders' sons holding the CEO position.

Back in the 1970s, both founders, with backgrounds in engineering and humanities, were fascinated by the potential of composite materials that could serve as an advanced alternative to traditional concrete, steel, aluminium and wood materials. The couple were looking for a technological process that would allow production of this technologically advanced substitute product on a relatively small scale. During a visit to Norway in 1978, they came across composite profiles that were made using the so-called pultrusion process. The term pultrusion combines the words pull and extrusion. The extrusion method entails the pushing of material through a shaped die, while pultrusion is based on the pulling of material, such as fibreglass, through a shaped die. Their fascination for this method was so extensive that the couple decided to start their own company, which would not only produce composite profiles, but also seek opportunities to develop and improve the technology.

The first profiles were drawn through pultrusion lines installed at rented premises in the founders' home town and shortly after they hired their first two employees. However, the company faced many challenges ahead, because it had an unknown product, with an immature process and a market that did not exist. But the founders never doubted it was worthwhile. As one of them recalled: 'After we started, we had seven very thin years, but we consoled ourselves with the fact that seven fat years may be waiting us ahead.'

5.2.2 Progress Tracking

This determination indeed paid off, as initially slow growth accelerated dramatically in the mid-1980s, allowing the company to assume ownership of the buildings it had been renting. By the late 1980s, Alpha was employing 15 employees. However, many challenges remained. The main one was related to finding markets for the composite profiles. Challenging the monopoly of steel and aluminium in the rather conservative construction industry was not easy. In retrospect, it was quite ironic considering the fact that characteristics of composites were making them more competitive than the traditional alternatives. But the industry needed to be convinced.

To respond to this, in the early 1990s, Alpha invested heavily in developing a design manual that would serve as a reference for customers. Parts of the manual were developed together with a network of Alpha's customers as a tool that made it faster and easier to design and create effective pultruded profile structures based on the company's products. This tool was also meant to ease and help facilitate the dialogue between Alpha's specialists and customers when it came to projects that required customized solutions.

In the 1990s, the company continued to grow and the need for more production capacity became obvious. In 1997, Alpha opened a new manufacturing facility, and the year 1997 signified another milestone in the company's history. In addition to the design manual, the founders decided to make the composite material better known in wider circles, not least among architects and designers. Alpha offered to build the first composite bridge in Scandinavia. The 'plastic' bridge made the press headlines and placed Alpha prominently on the map as well as attracting international attention. Since then, the company has been involved in many international projects. These include the Pontresina bridge and the Eyecatcher building in Switzerland, the bridge across the high-speed railway line between Madrid and Barcelona and the high-way bridge in Oxfordshire, UK.

However, the construction industry was not the only industry the company was targeting with its unique technology. Experience and expertise with composite materials enabled the company to develop and deliver unique solutions for the wind turbine industry as well. Alpha made its first steps in this market in the 1990s. The company's profiles were used in the construction of wind turbines and wind turbine blades. Glass fibre reinforced plastics (GRP) are non-corrosive and combine high strength with low weight. Therefore, profiles made with GRP provided a very good alternative to conventional structural materials such as concrete, steel and aluminium widely used in the industry.

In 2007, the company's headquarters and the main production facilities were moved to a newly built site. The company invested more than 25 million euros in the site, which would become one of the most advanced facilities for the pultrusion processes in Europe. It incorporated the latest advancements of industrial design and was significantly larger than the old factories. The size of the new site was approximately 23 000 m². The new production and office building was designed to be an efficient, functional workplace. The production layout lent itself to swift and even production flow with the input of raw materials at one end of the building, the pultrusion lines in the middle and the machining functions and warehouse at the other end. At the same time the building was attractive and inspiring architecturally and was supposed to represent and symbolize the founders' visions and values. The high roof space and extensive use of glass ensured the feeling of openness, transparency and connectedness.

Environmental sustainability was another key focus area for Alpha. Alpha's electricity consumption went into reverse as early as 2000, when the company's own wind turbine put 30 per cent more power into the grid than the company actually used. In 2010, the company became one of the first European enterprises to pre-process composites for recycling and use them as a substitute fuel and raw material for cement production.

The positive trajectory of the company's development was also reflected in the growing number of employees. From 2001 to 2011, it increased from 100 to 140, with approximately half involved in production and the other half employed in white-collar positions. The research and development (R&D) department played an especially important role in the company's activities, not only being at the forefront of Alpha's own innovation projects, but also coordinating collaborative initiatives with customers, universities and research centres from all over Europe.

5.2.3 Markets, Products and Technology

The brief description of the development path showed that Alpha started with its founders' vision to build a business based on innovation and continuous improvement of technology. Therefore, right from inception, the company was characterized by high knowledge intensity and the drive to exploit innovative opportunities in many industrial sectors. The company relied on different types of knowledge, including market, technological and business knowledge.

As mentioned above, Alpha focused on the wind energy and construction industries. Within these industries it covered three main market segments: (1) wind power; (2) construction profiles; and (3) windows, door and facade solutions. This rather structured approach was developed as part of a strategy that dated back to 2006. As part of this, the company decided to have a more structured approach to its markets and competence areas. As the head of business development recalled, '4–5 years ago we had to look at what we are really good at and where the growth opportunities are on the market and how we will capture these opportunities. We realized that if we are only good at technology but cannot turn it into profit; we will soon be out of business. Such an analysis lasted almost a year and resulted in the three primary focus segments: wind energy, construction, and window, facade and door profiles.'

Ready-to-install modules for the wind power industry included customer-specific reinforcement profiles and gratings for turbine blades, wind turbine towers and nacelles. In the wind power segment, Alpha also provided finished components and structures, including service and offshore platforms, helihoists and boat landings. In the construction segment, the company offered structural profiles and brackets, which served as an alternative to traditional materials. The company also produced profiles and decks for bridges, planks for application in walking areas and profiles for cooling towers, as well as window, door and facade profiles offering superior performance parameters. For example, Alpha's window profiles provided significantly better thermo isolation than analogues made with traditional materials.

The three market segments were very different. Therefore, a firm grip on their developments and a differentiated approach was the key to capturing current and future customer needs. The construction segment was the most competitive. The reason for this was that most of the pultrusion companies were targeting this segment, providing profile structures for big infrastructure projects. The window and door segment was one of the markets with the greatest potential. According to the business development manager, 'If we could capture a fraction of the market of aluminium frames, our factory would not even have the capacity to satisfy the demand.'

However, it goes without saying that without its technological knowledge and expertise, Alpha would not have been able to compete in any of the three market segments. Its technological knowledge was generated over the course of many years and thanks to the founders' passion for engineering and creativity. It seemed that composites, which constituted the core of Alpha's technology, provided a perfect base for experimentation and the development of new innovative solutions. Composites are defined as materials that consist of at least two different component materials, neither of which are well suited for construction purposes on their own, but which in a unique combination result in a very strong and rigid material. Alpha focused on plastics reinforced with synthetic materials reinforced with long continual fibres. When using composite materials instead of traditional materials, such as steel or aluminium, for example, there is normally a significant reduction in weight due to (a) the specific properties of the individual components and (b) the possibility of producing composites for specific purposes. A composite product can be combined and designed to accommodate specific load-bearing capacities, while providing a number of advantages, such as resistance to chemicals, as well as electrical and thermal insulating properties. Although products made with composite materials are more expensive, they require less maintenance, which makes them an attractive long-term investment.

Capturing all of these characteristics and communicating them to the market was part of the business acumen of the founders, who managed to create an organization capable of finding its niche in the market and dealing with the uncertainties and risks of the daily business environment.

5.2.4 Alpha's International Expansion

As mentioned above, the company's brand new site opened in 2007. There were several reasons to make a significant investment into these new facilities at the domestic base. First, Alpha intended to keep the core of its activities in Europe. Second, the company held a firm belief that production had a future in Europe, where some of the company's markets remained very lucrative. This was especially true for the window profiles market, which could also be characterized by specific national requirements and which required production proximity to the market.

However, in the wind turbine sector, the 'winds were shifting'. Alpha, a niche player that supplied very specific components to this highly consolidated industry, found itself very dependent upon its large customers. These customers were actively seeking ways to enhance their position in the Asian market. Many of them also faced local content requirements for projects in China. To respond to these trends, in 2009, Alpha had no other choice but to establish its own site in China. It would become its first operations base outside the home base in Europe. As a business development manager noted, 'If we were to stay in the wind sector, we needed to have presence in Asia'.

The site was a green-field investment. The reason for this was the uniqueness of Alpha's technology and the limited potential for synergies from acquisitions of local companies. The size of the factory in China was approximately 5000 m². In the first quarter of 2011, it employed nine blue-collar workers and three administrative staff. By 2013, the company plans to establish its local sales, sourcing and engineering departments and have 35 employees in China.

The production manager in China described the process the company went through in establishing the site as 'quite organic and driven by the founders' family vision rather than by a strict pre-defined plan'. Since the establishment process began in 2009, the start-up process in China has been closely overseen from the headquarters in Europe. An expat general manager was dispatched to China to manage the process and assist a local production manager. After one year, in 2010, the positions were swapped; that is the local production manager was promoted to the general manager's position, and the expat manager became the production manager. This was a very important decision that empowered the local manager and established a balanced, constructive relationship between the expat manager and the local general manager. According to the local general manager, 'We learn a lot from each other and have a very open relationship, which benefits us and the company.' This also helped to change the 'parent–child' type relationship that had formed between the headquarters and the Chinese site and made it more equal. However, the role of the headquarters in decision making remained very important.

The business development manager commented on the particular approach to enter China: 'As far as China is concerned, acquisition has never really been an option for us. We were in the position financially to acquire a Chinese company with similar technology. But similar doesn't mean the same. We have quite a few unique processes and we weren't sure that we would benefit from acquiring something as opposed to starting it from scratch.' The green-field approach also helped to ensure that all Alpha's environmental, quality and recruitment policies and standards were meticulously followed.

At the initial stages of establishment in China, Alpha only served its Western customers. Undoubtedly, the existing customer base was important to Alpha. However, longer-term ambitions included establishing closer collaboration with an indigenous Chinese customer base and developing a product range that would serve their needs, thereby reducing dependency on the company's Western customers and helping Alpha to become a more flexible multi-visional firm.

In the process of establishing a local customer base, Alpha faced a number of challenges. First, some challenges were related to the fact that the company was a new, very small player facing fierce competition on the Chinese market. Second, knowledge and innovation from individual projects could not easily be transferred between projects, as customers were very protective of their products. As the site general manager in China noted: 'All customers are very protective of their technology. If we do something customized, we of course cannot take the solution and transfer it to one of their competitors.' This meant that for every new customer, the company had to start almost from scratch. Third, in order to be competitive on the Chinese market, Alpha also needed to establish and enhance stable upstream supply chain linkages with local glass and resin suppliers. As the business development manager commented: 'In a country like China, we need our own organization with local supply base competitive on the Chinese terms ... If we only have some suppliers who only deal with other Western companies it may not be enough.' Fourth, Alpha's prices were considerably higher than their Chinese competitors' prices. Alpha saw all these issues as serious, but not detrimental to its long-term prospects on the Chinese market. The optimism was based on the belief that superior quality and compliance with environmental standards were increasingly valued by the market and encouraged by the government. Furthermore, Alpha's management was confident in the strength of the company's technological know-how. According to the local general manager, 'Our products are based on quality and the bank of knowledge and technological expertise defining our company.'

One of the lessons the company learned almost from the inception of being on the Chinese market was that in order to succeed, it had to develop a mindset that suited the local environment. The local Alpha organization in China focused on this task and was actively involved in the search for local suppliers. However, with very limited manpower and lots of activities coordinated with the European headquarters, it was a very time-consuming exercise. The results showed that a qualified supply base capable of complying with Alpha's standards was quite scarce in China. This posed a real short- and mid-term challenge, which had to be overcome if all materials and external services for the Chinese site were to be sourced from the Chinese supply base.

In the first quarter of 2011, the site in China did not have any pultrusion processes. It seemed that the establishment process took longer than initially anticipated. Therefore, all of the materials were shipped from Europe to China for processing and then distributed to customers in China. The first parallel production line was moved to China in the autumn of 2011. This first production line outside the home base enabled the company to produce the same components in China and draw upon the advantage of lower production cost, transport savings and proximity to the Chinese market. As the company started to produce in China, the site was still in a very 'fluid' state and was 'building the bridge as it was walking on it'. The continuous changes were related to the integration of new suppliers, training local employees, adjustments in the production processes and their alignment with the processes in Europe. The smooth transfer of production capabilities from Europe to China posed a serious challenge, as it was affected by a number of distances (for example, geographic, economic, cultural and administrative). The lack of local sales and sales support, sourcing and engineering units and the need to rely on the European base was also slowing down the process.

Alpha also emphasized the aspects of protecting intellectual property rights. Despite being very careful with how it dealt with applying its technology at its new base in China, the company still encountered cases in which local Chinese manufacturers were trying to copy products and take the market share. This fact only reinforced the founders' decision to keep the core of innovation and product development functions at the company's European home base. This was a way for Alpha to protect one of its major innovations – Alpha's pultrusion machine, which was developed and assembled internally in Europe. A site manager in China explained Alpha's rather conservative approach: 'Some can call our approach to China slow, outdated or even paranoid. But so far it helped us to avoid having a new competitor at every street corner.'

At the time the study was conducted in 2011, the Chinese competition did not have the same quality and specifications. In fact, according to Alpha's estimates, nine out of ten Asian competitors would not meet the quality standards required by their Western customers. However, there was a worrying trend: Chinese and South Korean manufacturers were catching up very fast and were very comfortable in their home markets. If not in terms of quality, but in terms of completeness of solutions, they were able to provide very similar systems at more competitive prices. Some of the big shipbuilding companies, such as Daewoo and Hyundai, were expanding into the wind turbine industry. This created both opportunities and threats. On the one hand, they could be potential future customers. On the other hand, there was the risk of competition from these giants.

5.3 WHAT HAVE WE LEARNED?

This case study describes Alpha's journey into international expansion of operations in four parts. The first part describes how it all began for Alpha and where the roots of its identity are. The second part presents the chronological development trajectory of the company. The third part focuses on the company's key markets and technologies. The first three parts provide initial inputs for understanding the rationales behind Alpha's decision to expand its international operations through a production start-up in China. The fourth part centres on unpacking how the green-field site in China was established and why this particular approach was chosen.

While the case is broad in its scope, it provides an opportunity to go into details on the following interrelated questions:

Why and how does a KIE venture apply its knowledge resources globally?

What are the main factors and determinants of such an application?

Alpha represents an example of a European KIE venture that is striving to apply its knowledge resources globally, despite its lack of international operations experience, scarce managerial resources and other challenges normally faced by KIE ventures at the establishment phase. There may be several explanations for this decision. First of all, powerful forces of globalization support or rather push the KIE into a global deployment of knowledge for rapid development. Facing intense global competition, in growing numbers, companies are seeking to achieve a higher degree of efficiency and effectiveness by configuring their activities on a global scale and utilizing the best locations for these activities (Mudambi, 2008). Some research seems to suggest that any kind of work can take place wherever the right technologies, skills and knowledge can be found (Doh, 2005). As a result, not only routine transactional tasks, but also more knowledge intensive and proprietary tasks are increasingly subject to global dispersion and fragmentation (De Vita and Wang, 2006; Lewin and Couto, 2007).

With regard to location choices, it seems that there is no one single motive for why Alpha chose China. By entering China, Alpha seeks to establish a position from which it can best exploit and at the same time explore new resources. By all means, it plans to establish and operate its unit in China to capture a share of this growth market through both the existing and a new customer base (market seeking) and take advantage of inexpensive factory costs (efficiency seeking). Nonetheless, tapping into the local sourcing market and the advanced technologies originating from this fast-developing context is also on the company's agenda (knowledge and strategic asset seeking).

According to the Economist Intelligence Unit (2012), the organizational structures most often used for entering China are: (1) the wholly foreign-owned venture (WFO); (2) the equity joint venture (EJV); and (3) the contractual or cooperative venture (CV). Relying on external partners is becoming an increasingly widespread strategy (Aron and Singh, 2005). This 'footloose' mode has a number of advantages in terms of flexibility, as well as lower risks than those associated with the investment required in the 'rooted' intrafirm scenario (Ferdows, 2008). In 2009, new measures were introduced in China that made it easier for foreign companies to enter into partnerships with Chinese companies. In spite of this, Alpha dismissed the EJV option, once China's most common investment vehicle, and other cooperative arrangements with Chinese partners with strong connections and direct knowledge of the market that could have been invaluable to a foreign company that was new to the market.

Instead, in Alpha the process of international expansion of operations occurs on an 'intrafirm' basis and it establishes a WFO venture. Keeping in mind that Alpha did not have any sales representation or export to China, their strategy was rather counterintuitive for SMEs entering China and different from what might have been expected according to traditional internationalization theory (Johanson and Vahlne, 1977).

The explanation for the rationale behind Alpha's chosen approach is several fold. First, its founders were concerned about the values of quality, innovation and environmental sustainability that defined Alpha from the venture's inception. The fear was that by engaging with local partners through EJV or acquisition, some of these core values might be compromised. Second, the WFO venture form provided Alpha with a high degree of independence. Third, and perhaps most importantly, various types of knowledge that characterize Alpha carried significant organizational and operational implications, which determined the mode of Alpha's operations expansion.

According to Almor et al. (2006), knowledge intensity is closely related to firm-specific knowledge. Alpha did all it could to maintain full control over its venture in China and to protect its knowledge assets from competitors. However, such a structure for the application of knowledge intensive resources across national borders also entailed significant costs and is certainly not a panacea against all challenges. The fact that it took Alpha almost two years to get the site in China up and running shows the enormity of the task that can be expected by KIE ventures planning to embark on similar journeys.

5.4 QUESTIONS FOR FURTHER REFLECTION

Describe Alpha's international development strategy. Discuss alternative ways of internationalizing operations and applying knowledge resources globally.

What are the main advantages and disadvantages of Alpha's international development strategy?

Contrast and compare Alpha's start-up in China with KIE venturing.

Discuss possible future international development scenarios at Alpha Composites. What are the main driving forces and impediments in each case?

REFERENCES

Almor, T., N. Hashai and S. Hirsch (2006), 'The product cycle revisited: knowledge intensity and firm internationalization', *Management International Review*, **46** (5), 507–28.

Aron, R. and J.V. Singh (2005), 'Getting offshoring right', *Harvard Business Review*, **83** (12), 135–43.

De Vita, G. and C.L. Wang (2006), 'Development of outsourcing theory and practice: a taxonomy of outsourcing generations', in H.S. Kehal and V.P. Singh (eds), *Outsourcing and Offshoring in the 21st Century: A Socio-economic Perspective*, Hershey, PA: Idea Group Publishing, pp. 1–17.

Doh, J.P. (2005), 'Offshore outsourcing: implications for international business and strategic management theory and practice', *Journal of Management Studies*, **42** (3), 695–704.

Economist Intelligence Unit (2012), *Organising an Investment in China: Prepare for Opportunity*, London: The Economist.

Ferdows, K. (2008), 'Managing the evolving global production network', in R. Galavan, J. Murray and C. Markides (eds), *Strategy, Innovation, and Change: Challenges for Management*, Oxford: Oxford University Press, pp. 149–62.

Johanson, J. and J.E. Vahlne (1977), 'The internationalisation process of the firm – a model of knowledge development and increasing foreign market commitments', *Journal of International Business Studies*, **8** (1), 23–32.

Lewin, A.Y. and V. Couto (2007), *Offshoring Research Network 2006 Survey Report: Next Generation Offshoring – The Globalization of Innovation*, Chicago, IL: Booz Allen Hamilton.

Mudambi, R. (2008), 'Location, control and innovation in knowledge-intensive industries', *Journal of Economic Geography*, **8** (2), 699–725.

6. The nexus between technology, organizational and market development: the case of NanoSpace Inc.

Astrid Heidemann Lassen

6.1 SETTING THE STAGE

A common characteristic of knowledge intensive entrepreneurship (KIE) firms is the desire to pursue a detected opportunity, but often with a lack of necessary resources to do so. In this connection, the value of networks is widely acknowledged in the literature (for example, Aldrich and Zimmer, 1986; Hite and Hesterly, 2001). Networking is considered a system by which entrepreneurs can tap into resources that are external to them, that is, resources over which they have no direct control. In its simplest form, networking consists of the use of all personal relationships to obtain advice, financing, sales and so on. In its most sophisticated form, entrepreneurs make use of elaborate webs of relationships between companies, which makes them extremely efficient and flexible at delivering a product or service to the market. As such, networking is an important topic in relation to KIE; and evidence suggests that the process of managing KIE ventures is strongly affected by the network activities of these ventures.

In this case study we see how leveraging networks in a KIE venture is a way to overcome problems related to resources, knowledge and legitimacy alike. In particular, in KIE ventures, the entrepreneurial activities and the importance of networks are not only related to the development of the venture itself. As we illustrate in the case of NanoSpace Inc., the entrepreneurial use of networks is equally significant for developing an immature market and technology as well as further developing the immature organization.

As such, the questions addressed through the case study are: how and why do networks affect the recognition and realization of innovative opportunities?

6.2 THE CASE OF NANOSPACE INC.

The first satellite launched was the Soviet Sputnik 1 on 1 October 1957. The payload on this satellite was a radio transmitter that could transmit temperature measurements from inside and outside the satellite. The following year, the USA launched the Explorer 1 satellite. This satellite payload was a tape that played Christmas greetings that were transmitted back to Earth. These two satellites marked the beginning of satellite development.

Satellite development, at this early stage, was an expensive process supported only by large countries. The satellites were also very limited in the functionality they offered. Quickly, satellite development moved into a commercial industry where the 'Early Bird' was the first commercially launched satellite. It was launched by the then Hughes Aircraft Company that has now become Boeing Satellite Systems. This satellite opened the first satellite communications channel between Europe and the USA. A large satellite industry has since been built in different parts of the world, and over the past 50 years, the uses for satellites have been many. The primary use of satellites up until the 1980s was for communications and military purposes. Later some military functions like the Global Positioning System (GPS) were commercialized and a wider range of applications and services were developed (Pedersen, 2011).

In recent years, CubeSat technology has emerged within the satellite industry. A CubeSat (short for Cubic Satellite) is a miniaturized satellite, which was initially developed as part of a research project started at Stanford University in the USA. The CubeSat is today used in academic projects at many universities around the world. The CubeSat project was started in order to investigate the possibilities of simplifying the general satellite infrastructure, making it cheaper to produce basic satellites. Developing a cheap and small satellite would open up many new areas of application, where traditional large-scale, highly expensive satellites vastly overshoot the needs of the market.

A CubeSat holds four main applications: (1) beep-sats, for educational research satellites; (2) scientific missions, for technical measurements; (3) technology missions, for technology tests in space; and (4) communication, for radio and picture transmission.

Due to the fact that CubeSat technology emerged based on university research projects, a common standard has emerged in order for the different research projects to be able to compare results of size and mass, as well as share launches. This is a distinct advantage developed due to the tight network structure of the academic environment in the field. As a result of these standards of interfaces on the CubeSat, it is now easy and cheap to arrange launches. The standards define that the satellite is always 10 cm³ and weighs less than 1.3 kg, which means that there is no need for facilitating each individual satellite.

A complete CubeSat satellite system can be purchased at around 150 000 euros. This is a very significant cost reduction in comparison to, for example, the costs of the Oersted Satellite, launched in 1999, priced at approximately 25 000 000 euros, considered a very cheap large satellite or compared to the contemporary standard price range of around 285 000 000 euros.

NanoSpace Inc. is an academic spin-off company established in 2007. The university home to the founders of NanoSpace Inc. have been part of the international CubeSat initiative since the early 2000s, and have had three successful launches. This makes the university amongst the world leading research environments within the field.

NanoSpace Inc. develops, manufactures and sells various subsystems and complete solutions for CubeSat space missions. It is an entrepreneurial company, based on the experience gained by the founders while doing research and development at the university. NanoSpace Inc. is determined to introduce solutions and systems that will unlock the technological potential and commercial opportunities of CubeSats. Their strategy is demonstrated here.

It is our vision that NanoSpace Inc. in 2015 maintains a leading position as a driving force in the emerging market for nano-satellites and demonstrates new applications of nanosats. Our products and services will help teams across the globe to realize their goals in space.

Mission: NanoSpace Inc. will develop the global market for space systems and services by introducing new products, i.e. components, platforms and systems, based on innovation within CubeSat technology.

Goals: To build legitimacy around NanoSpace Inc. products and capabilities, and through this, increase sales and awareness of NanoSpace Inc. products.

Strategy: Use the existing networks to develop collaboration to achieve growth using the strong product portfolio of NanoSpace Inc.

This strategy very clearly signals a number of areas that need development. These include the technology (the understanding of the potential directions of technology development), the market and business potential, and the organizational set-up of NanoSpace Inc. It is also highly apparent that the entrepreneurs are aware that the way to go about creating such developments is dependent on their ability to successfully utilize networks.

6.2.1   Venturing in Immature Markets through Networks

In order to understand how NanoSpace Inc. utilizes its network, and why this is such an important feature of the venture strategy, one must first understand the conditions of the CubeSat market.

The CubeSat market it still in its infancy, which means that neither the companies nor customers have been completely defined. Since 2003, 57 CubeSats have been launched in the world. Of these 57, 28 have been launched in the USA by different types of organizations. This averages to three satellites being launched every year. From the 25 US satellites, 17 have been launched by universities, 8 by a space agency and 3 were purely commercial (Pedersen, 2011). This shows that the commercial market of NanoSpace Inc. is still very limited, and only a handful of players are significant in this industry.

In relation to dealing with the challenge of market immaturity, NanoSpace Inc. has chosen a proactive path. The market development is being done in close collaboration with the three major competitors in the field. The three major competitors of NanoSpace Inc. are IBiS from the Netherlands, ClydeSpace from Scotland and Pumpkin from California, USA.

There are no major differences between NanoSpace Inc. and its three competitors. However, the four are believed to possess different areas of expertise and they may in fact benefit from each other. The fact that NanoSpace Inc. is able to deliver the entire palate is considered a competitive edge. The other competitors are not able to deliver complete satellite systems as a finished high quality platform. As the market matures it will become evident whether a strategy of specialization or complete solutions is the best fit for the market.

The four players all have fewer than 30 employees and none have a particular specialty that makes them distinct from the others. Within the industry there is a price focus, which may eventually force the four to battle each other in an intense race of elimination. This is, however, not the case at the moment, because large growth rates are expected within the market in the coming years. As a result of this, none of the players have been forced to compete for market shares. Instead the focus is to a high degree on how to collaboratively develop the market to the extent where all can start profiting substantially. The four players have realized that in order to benefit from the market, there is a need to educate the market on the advantages of the technology they all have in common. The roles within the network for developing the market have not been clearly defined between the players. Therefore, no streamlined strategy to develop the market has been developed. Business developer, Soren Petersen at NanoSpace Inc. describes the situation as follows:

> You could compare it to a very elaborate Domino Effect. Every aspect of the industry and technology is dependent on the steps that go before, and will directly influence the possible steps to come. It's like the PC market in the 1980s, and it is happening very fast. So we need to continuously evaluate what the current possibilities are at this precise moment, and which new steps recent developments and activities open up for.

> As such, it becomes evident that a network approach to the other actors in the market is essential. Not only as a means to access resources or legitimacy, but also a tool for synergetic development of the market in a way that is beyond what any of the players are capable of accomplishing individually.

6.2.2 Emerging Network Value Chain

The immaturity of the market is also visible in the construction of the value chain of NanoSpace Inc., which is highly dynamic and subject to continuous change in relations.

As depicted in Figure 6.1, part of the upstream value chain is characterized by standard supplier/buyer relationships, as NanoSpace Inc. has a number of suppliers, for example, mechanical, electronic and photovoltaic, which are components of their system. Such components are fairly standard and used in a variety of different settings, showing that the suppliers are also well-established and mature organizations.

However, this is where the similarities to mature supply chains ends. As a part of the upstream relationships we find two of the competitors of NanoSpace Inc. This indicates that in spite of being direct competitors on some aspects, Pumpkin, IBiS and NanoSpace Inc. also support each other through joint business activities.

At the downstream end of the value chain, we also see atypical constellations. Here NanoSpace Inc. acts as a supplier for otherwise competitors IBiS and ClydeSpace, while also trading directly with a number of end customers. Chief Executive Officer (CEO) Larry Larson explains the situation like this:

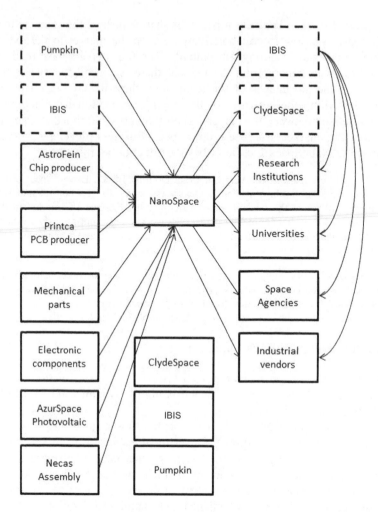

Figure 6.1   Value chain of NanoSpace Inc.

We are and have always been very focused on developing the technology, whereas for instance IBiS has been much more focused on the market side. Their access to the end-consumer is very strong and they protect these relations very well. So, this means that in relation to such customers we are necessarily positioned as supplier through IBiS. We know that this is not an optimal situation. IBiS also has development activities, so at some point they will start pushing their own products rather than ours. So, we need to start establishing more direct customer relationships to hedge this risk. But, we should also keep in mind that a significant share of our current sales are through IBiS at this point – so it's a difficult intertwined issue to deal with.

In this sense, the immaturity of the market and lack of cementation of clear roles means that the different actors simultaneously have several different types of relationships to each other. They realize the risks involved in this, but are also aware that in order to advance the technology and markets sufficiently, these are the current operating circumstances under which they have to act.

The end customers are all actors highly dependent on public/institutional funding. Even the industrial vendors are dependent on associations with publically funded projects. This makes the market rather unstable, and highly dependent on the political agenda for allocation of public funding to space research.

In spite of this instability, NanoSpace Inc. has been subject to extreme growth in the past years. In 2011, NanoSpace Inc. grew by 300 per cent, and over the past two years NanoSpace Inc. has grown by approximately 700 per cent in revenue. Despite this realized growth, the future is still expected to hold great opportunities. Currently, NanoSpace Inc. participates in around 14 satellite projects per year. In 2012, the venture had 60 systems being launched from nine different countries, and the numbers are expected to grow. However, the diversity and immaturity of stable features in the market are clearly reflected in the sales figures of NanoSpace Inc. In 2011 the distribution in revenue based activity was as follows: full platforms sales 23 per cent, satellite subsystems sales 20 per cent, consulting and European Space Agency (ESA) work 26 per cent, grant based development 31 per cent.

The sale of platform solutions and satellite subsystems is considered the core business and is also a growing part of the total revenue generated. However, at the time of writing it actually accounts for less than half of the revenue generated.

The consulting and ESA work are not core products of NanoSpace Inc., but can both still be used as ways of demonstrating technical capabilities in the company to thereby attract new customers. It can also be used as a way of maintaining cash flow while applying the specific space based properties and know-how built into the company.

Finally, the largest source of income for NanoSpace Inc. in both 2010 and 2011 has been through grant based development work. This has been composed of projects, like the Automatic Dependent Surveillance-Broadcast based (ADS-B) project that NanoSpace Inc. was involved in. This was a development project for monitoring commercial air traffic funded by the Advanced Technology Foundation.

6.2.3   Interrelatedness of Network Relations

NanoSpace Inc. is currently engaging in activities worldwide, with the most recent specific initiatives in Asia, Israel and Germany. However, the primary market potential for NanoSpace Inc.'s products is still considered to be in the USA. This is due to the fact that the USA is relatively more advanced in the potential areas of application for satellite technology, and has proved more willing to invest in pilot projects. As such, several initiatives to penetrate this market are currently being undertaken. This can be seen directly through the networking activities that serve as a good example of how the networks are used in a dynamic and inter-related manner in order to simultaneously develop the market, the technology and the potential of NanoSpace Inc. for conducting business.

NanoSpace Inc. has no less than six distinctive collaborative network connections related to the US market. These networks vary in nature, some being more specific than others. The benefits of the networks vary from technological expertise over personal relations to market insights. The latter is especially important to NanoSpace Inc.

The US network consists of possible suppliers and customers of NanoSpace Inc. The supplier/customer relations are, however, not as clear-cut as in more established industries. In the CubeSat industry, the same actor could potentially be a supplier, customer and broker to new opportunities at different points in time. Hence, the approach to the actors also needs to be very diverse and not only reliant on contractual agreements.

The collaboration with Stinger Graffarian Technologies (SGT) is based upon a social relationship between a STG employee and the founders of NanoSpace Inc. The dyadic network relation has served as a way of attaining knowledge and contacts. The relationship between SGT and NanoSpace Inc. is very general and based on mutual trust. This can be explained by the social nature of the relationship.

The collaboration with Stanford University entails and opens up many important contacts within the space based environment of the USA. Their main contact is however, not willing to enter into a trust based collaborative relationship with NanoSpace Inc. This is because the contact does not perceive benefits as sufficient to develop a general collaboration. Since the contact does not want general collaboration, its services can only be acquired for specific tasks that NanoSpace Inc. will have to be willing to pay for.

The collaboration with Pumpkin is a technology connection. Furthermore, the network relationship in the future will most likely include Pumpkin distributing NanoSpace Inc. products. NanoSpace Inc. is, however, wary of establishing too strong network ties to Pumpkin, as they are considered to lack integrity in the US market. This lack of integrity could become associated with NanoSpace Inc. if the network relation were to be expanded. Therefore, the relationship is based on informal understandings of the collaboration.

California Polytechnic University (CPU) is the leading CubeSat university. In more mature markets you would normally not consider a university to be a part of the industry. However, in the CubeSat industry universities are actually a large part of the customer base, in addition to being essential network partners in relation to the knowledge development. Hence, they are important parts of the immature industry. Despite the possible sales relationship, the contact at CPU contributes mostly to the technological development of NanoSpace Inc., and not its direct growth. As a partner in the NanoSpace network, the university has very high esteem within the industry and this is a very valuable contact in relation to brokering access to high profile research projects and collaborations with large players, such as the National Aeronautics and Space Administration (NASA).

The collaboration with NASA is based on specific projects. It is the intention that NanoSpace Inc. is to provide the platform and NASA will produce any mission specific payload. The collaboration between Nano-Space Inc. and NASA is not balanced however. The power is very much in favour of NASA. On the other hand, NanoSpace Inc. may be able to attain legitimacy and status from their collaboration with NASA, working with them at the pinnacle of space development.

The Naval Postgraduate School (NPS) is included as a specific collaborator. NPS is a customer of NanoSpace Inc. This is, however, not the fundamental relationship. At the core of the collaboration is a professor at NPS, who has extremely high integrity within the industry. As a customer, NPS buys specific NanoSpace Inc. products. In addition, the contact provides feedback for NanoSpace Inc. about the products. Because of his integrity, his product validation is a great asset for NanoSpace Inc. The network actors and their relations are depicted in Figure 6.2.

What this picture of the network activities in the markets shows us is a complex and dynamic structure, which relies on the ability of NanoSpace Inc. to be able to navigate between general and specific collaboration, as well as social and industry related networks. As described, a number of overlaps exist between the social and industry related networks, with the view being primarily of the division into general and specific collaborations being used as a guideline by NanoSpace Inc.

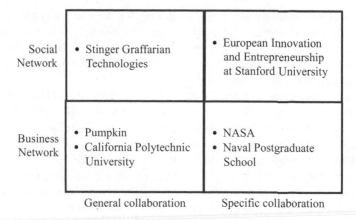

	General collaboration	Specific collaboration
Social Network	• Stinger Graffarian Technologies	• European Innovation and Entrepreneurship at Stanford University
Business Network	• Pumpkin • California Polytechnic University	• NASA • Naval Postgraduate School

Figure 6.2   Primary market network actors

6.2.4   Network Influence on the NanoSpace Organization

Not only are the market aspects of NanoSpace Inc. immature, the organization itself is also very young and immature. In this section we focus on how networks and networking have a significant influence on the ability to develop the organization of NanoSpace Inc.

Three entrepreneurs, Larry Larson, Carl Cage and Matthew Monroe, founded NanoSpace Inc. All of the three founders hold as a minimum a Master's degree with a specialty in intelligent autonomous systems. Table 6.1 elaborates the individual founder's titles and characteristics.

The founders know each other from the research projects they participated in during their education at university, and use their common background as a frame of reference for discussing network contacts and future employees; in addition to, of course, the technological features of the products. As such, the link to the common academic network is still very actively used as part of their organizational development.

Alongside financial growth, NanoSpace Inc. has over the past year increased its staff from the three entrepreneurs to six full-time employees. The high level of education has, however, been sustained throughout the expansion and enabled NanoSpace Inc. to sustain its technological position in the market.

The educational backgrounds of the entrepreneurs and employees allows for great specialization within the technology development area, which is not easily transferred to managerial competences. Thus, in the early years of NanoSpace Inc., the focus on sales and business development was

Table 6.1   Founder characteristics

Name	Larry Larson	Carl Cage	Matthew Monroe
Title	Managing Director	Space Projects Manager	Senior Engineer
Degrees	MSc EE with specialty in intelligent autonomous systems, and holds a PhD degree in advanced model based methods for control and estimation	MSc EE with specialty in intelligent autonomous systems	MSc EE with specialty in intelligent autonomous systems, and holds a PhD degree in advanced modelling and control of autonomous helicopters
Field of expertise	Systems engineering and model based control and sensor fusion	Electronic space applications and development and implementation of reliable software for mission critical applications	Modelling and simulation of motion control systems, instrumentation, advanced fusion techniques
Previous practice	Involved in the development and execution of both AAU-CubeSat and SSETI-Express	Lead architect for Command and Data-handling for the satellites: SSETI-Express, Bumanetz and AAUSAT-II; two years of research in estimation for hybrid systems	A driving force behind AAU-CubeSat; additionally, he was involved in SSETI-Express

limited. This was not necessarily a deliberate choice, but rather a natural consequence, reflected by the backgrounds and experiences of the founders. NanoSpace Inc. has, however, evolved and solved these initial challenges. In 2010, Soren Petersen was employed. He holds a Master's degree in international technology management. At NanoSpace Inc. Soren Petersen is employed as a business developer, in charge of both market analysis and sales. This employment was in direct continuation of an internship, where Soren spent several months in the USA, familiarizing himself with the players of this market, and establishing contacts for NanoSpace Inc. This employment strengthened the managerial competencies of NanoSpace Inc., especially in the sense that Soren Petersen has added a strategic aspect to the approach of establishing and utilizing networks. This is an important step in NanoSpace Inc.'s strategy.

As such, we can observe that in relation to the organizational development of NanoSpace Inc., the network relationships of the founders and employees play a very significant role in connection to the identification of new sources of knowledge.

6.3   WHAT HAVE WE LEARNED FROM NANOSPACE INC.?

Through this case study we have looked at several aspects related to how and why networks affect the recognition and realization of innovative opportunities.

In particular, we have seen how networks have been used in several distinct ways in order for the KIE venture to simultaneously engage in the development of the market, the technology and the organization. It has become evident that a network approach to the other actors in the market is essential. Not only as a means to access resources or legitimacy; but also a tool for synergetic development of the market in a way that is beyond what either of the players is capable of accomplishing individually.

One of the most striking aspects identified in this case study is the way in which the different actors simultaneously have several different types of relationships with each other. As such, networking activity in KIE ventures can be seen as a highly complex and dynamic structure, which builds equally on the personal relationships, the technological knowledge of the actors and the business possibilities accessible through the actors. The successful development of the venture relies on the ability to navigate between such different actors/relations.

At certain points in time the interrelatedness of the actors created somewhat unfavourable circumstances for the KIE venture, which were difficult to avoid. However, what we see is that the entrepreneurs actively weighed the risks and advantages of being so tightly knitted to the other actors in the network. Thereby, they were continuously preparing for engagement in a variety of different and new constellations as soon as the market, technology and organizational set-up were sufficiently developed.

This approach has a strong resemblance to design thinking, which emphasizes a particular proactive way of dealing with problems as systems of more or less related spaces, which can be manipulated in different ways, based on iterative processes of prototyping, testing and refinement.

In this way, the knowledge intensive entrepreneurs in NanoSpace Inc. design all aspects of the market, technology and organizational development. These networks are the means to enable the entrepreneurs to gain access to resources, gain legitimacy, extend the knowledge, educate the market, position themselves in connection to future possibilities, gain access to customers, source and sell and so on. This understanding highlights how KIE differs significantly from development in more mature markets, organizations and technology domains.

6.4 QUESTIONS FOR FURTHER REFLECTION

Discuss which skills are necessary to develop as a knowledge intensive entrepreneur in order to be able to navigate successfully in network governed markets like the one seen in the case of Nano-Space Inc.

Discuss how the use of networks will most likely change as a venture grows.

Which parallels/contrasts to what we have learned from the Nano-Space case can you identify in other industries?

What do you think are the most appropriate next steps for Nano-Space to take?

REFERENCES

Aldrich, H.E. and C. Zimmer (1986), 'Entrepreneurship through social networks', in D. Sexton and J. Kasarda (eds), *The Art and Science of Entrepreneurship*, Cambridge, MA: Ballinger, pp. 3–23.

Hite, J.M. and W.S. Hesterly (2001), 'The evolution of firm networks, from emergence to early growth of the firm', *Strategic Management Journal*, **22**, 275–86.

Pedersen, S. (2011), 'A network approach to market entry: a case study of an entrepreneurial company entering an emerging US market', Master's thesis, Aalborg University.

PART II

Lifestyle technologies

7. Knowledge intensive entrepreneurship from firm exit in a high-tech cluster: the case of the wireless communications cluster in Aalborg, Denmark

Christian Richter Østergaard and Eunkyung Park

7.1 INTRODUCTION

This chapter addresses how the existence of a cluster of firms with a specific knowledge base in a region affects future knowledge intensive entrepreneurship (KIE) in that region. Focusing on spinoff activities, the case of the wireless communication cluster in North Jutland in Denmark demonstrates how entrepreneurs develop knowledge, skills, routines, social capital and networks while working in an industry and then go on to use these resources to create new business in the same or related industries in the same approximate location.

Various studies show that spinoffs, firms established by entrepreneurs with prior experience gained from existing firms in the same industry, perform better than other types of start-ups (see, for example, Dahl and Reichstein, 2007). It is believed that when the founder has pre-entry experience in the industry, relevant routines, skills and knowledge are transferred from the incumbents to the new firms, providing a competitive advantage to spinoffs as compared to other entrants into the industry. Since spinoffs tend to locate close to the 'parent' companies and perform better than other entrants, spinoff activities often lead to the geographical clustering of firms. This means that the existing industry structure of a region may affect the development of that industry in that region in the future. Empirical studies of the semiconductor industry in Silicon Valley, automobile industry in Detroit, tyre industry in Akron and the high-tech cluster in Cambridge, UK illustrate this mechanism quite well (Garnsey and Heffernan, 2005; Buenstorf and Klepper, 2009; Klepper, 2010).

The main purpose of this chapter is to illustrate KIE following firm exit in a declining high-tech cluster. More specifically, it shows how the entrepreneurs' knowledge of markets, products, technologies, unmet customer demand, competitors, suppliers and skills gained from pre-entry experience affect their search for and utilization of new business opportunities. Unlike studies focusing on the spinoff activities that drive the formation of clusters, however, this chapter intends to take a closer look at spinoff activities in a declining cluster originating from company closure.

The chapter investigates KIE in the wireless communications cluster around the city of Aalborg in Northern Denmark.[1] The cluster consists of firms in the field of maritime communication and navigation, telecommunications and land-based satellite communications equipment, and mobile and cordless communication. This comprises a high-technology knowledge intensive industry characterized by fast technological change and a growing global market. The first company here was established back in the 1960s, but the main growth in the cluster occurred during the 1990s, when the 15 firms grew to 40. The cluster peaked in 2003 with 50 firms employing 4500 people. Recently, the turbulence in the global wireless communications industry coupled with financial crisis hit the cluster hard and caused downsizing and even exit of firms. This caused a widespread fear in the regional economy that the closure of many firms would lead to loss of well-paid jobs for highly educated persons. However, as we will show in this case study, the negative process also led to the establishment of new firms. In 2009, a research and development (R&D) subsidiary of Motorola located in the cluster closed down. About 275 employees were laid off, but at the same time 20 new firms were founded by former employees. The case to be studied in detail is the KIE following the closure of the Motorola subsidiary in the context of a declining cluster. It will describe how these firms were founded and explore relations in general between the previous company and the new firms. Then, one of the new firms is chosen for a more detailed description of this type of KIE. The key questions are:

How do the existing firms and knowledge base affect future KIE?

To what extent does knowledge diffusion take place through KIE from existing firms?

How did the entrepreneurs' pre-entry experiences influence their new venture?

What effect does KIE from firm exit in one industry have on other industries in the region?

7.2 THE CASE: KIE IN A HIGH-TECH CLUSTER FOLLOWING FIRM CLOSURE

This section starts with a brief history of the wireless communications cluster by way of an introduction to the past KIE pattern. There follows a description of KIE after the closure of Motorola in 2009. The rapidly changing landscape of the mobile communications industry in recent years and the process of closure will be presented before KIE by the spinoffs are described in detail.

7.2.1 Earlier Spinoff Activities in the Cluster

The development of the wireless communications cluster in Aalborg, Denmark was always highly characterized by spinoff activities. The very first firm in the cluster, S.P. Radio, had diversified into wireless communications equipment for maritime use (small- and medium sized-vessels) in the early 1960s. The company was very successful and its products were considered technologically more advanced than those of the few competitors at the time. In 1973, three engineers from S.P. Radio established the first spinoff company, Dancom, producing maritime communications equipment. In 1977, two engineers from Dancom founded Shipmate, which also produced radiophones for maritime use. Shipmate developed a very successful satellite navigation system in 1981 at a third of the cost of its competitors and subsequently grew from three employees to 200.

Dancom went through severe financial difficulties in the early 1980s and was restructured and renamed Dancall Radio in 1983. At the same time, the company diversified into the related market of onshore mobile communications. Dancall grew quickly in the 1980s following the opening of the market based on the new common Nordic standard for mobile telephony (NMT). The size of Dancall and its technological base in the growing market for mobile phones and other wireless communications technologies made it a main seedbed of KIE in this cluster. The firm went through several crises and owners, but continued through the 1990s and 2000s to be a key company in the cluster, with many of the local entrepreneurs in the industry coming from this company. Shipmate, meanwhile, also expanded into mobile communications with the purpose of exploiting the promising business opportunities in the new market, through the establishment of a company named Cetelco. Cetelco developed its first NMT phone in 1986 and began to develop and produce mobile phones for several European and East Asian countries. In the 1980s and early 1990s, several spinoffs arose from Dancall and Shipmate, such as Danish Marine Communication (1980), Ammcom (1986), T-COM (1987), BD consult (1988), LH Mobil Radio (1991) and Gatehouse (1992). The founders of these firms often list new market opportunities not followed by the parent company or disagreement with the company strategy as reasons for starting their own ventures.

In the late 1980s, the work on a common European standard for mobile telephony (GSM) began. Dancall and Cetelco established a joint venture, DC Development, to develop the basic modules of a GSM phone together with Aalborg University at the local science park, NOVI. DC Development succeeded in developing the basic technologies, and these parent companies were among the first to introduce a GSM phone in 1992. By this time Cetelco had more than 100 employees, but it faced financial problems and was gradually taken over by the German company Hagenuk in 1988–90. Dancall had grown to more than 600 employees by 1993, it too had financial difficulties and sold its cordless telephony division. The problems continued, however, and Dancall was taken over by Amstrad, and then, in 1997, was acquired by Bosch, which wanted to enter the industry and grew it to 1700 employees by 1999. A year later the company was split into two, with the production side sold to Flextronics and the R&D to Siemens.

The wireless communications cluster grew rapidly in the 1990s with its competences in the GSM standard attracting various types of start-ups, including parent spinoffs (spinoffs owned by existing companies), but which mainly represented multinational corporations (MNCs) acquiring local firms or making green-field investments. Motorola was one of the MNCs to create a subsidiary in the cluster so as to access the specialized knowledge of workers in mobile telecommunications technology there. The cluster started to decline when the new standard (3G) emerged, however, mainly due to a lack of competences in the new technologies. After the peak of 2003, the number of firms and employees in the cluster started to drop, a decrease that continued with the (ongoing) major changes in the industry and the financial crisis from 2007. The decline of the cluster intensified when Motorola and Texas Instruments closed down in 2009. At the time of writing, the cluster consists of 45 firms employing some 2300 people, together with a university and science park. The next section explains the changes in the industry that led to the Motorola closure.

7.2.2 Turbulence in the Mobile Communications Industry

The introduction of the iPhone and Android smartphones in 2007 and the subsequent rise of new competitors proved to be a disruption to the mobile phone industry. These were 'disruptive' technologies in the sense of significant changes in the basic technologies that effect an alteration of the pattern of the existing industry. Christensen (1997) describes the disruption as not necessarily brought about by the new technology itself, but often resulting from the new business models, applications or customers that follow the introduction of the new technology. The disruption often comes from new firms entering the industry and the outcome is often a shift of market leaders and location (Utterback, 1994). Apple's iPhone OS (iOS) and Google's Android operating system radically changed the industry. The iPhone was initially not considered to be a good product by many of the traditional mobile phone companies in terms of its functioning as a phone, but together with the new technology it managed to change the entire industry in the years that followed.

According to Gartner, the market shares of the mobile phone market in 2008 were: Nokia 38.6 per cent, Samsung 16.3 per cent, Motorola 8.7 per cent (dropping from 14.3 per cent in 2007), LG Electronics 8.4 per cent and Sony Ericsson 7.6 per cent, while Apple sold 11 417 500 units, or 0.93 per cent. In 2011, Nokia's overall market share of mobile phones had dropped to 23.8 per cent followed by Samsung (17.7 per cent), Apple (5 per cent) and LG Electronics (4.9 per cent), while Motorola had fallen to 2.3 per cent market share. The sale of smartphones reached 31 per cent of the total number of mobile phones sold in 2011. The dominating operating system in the fourth quarter of 2011 was Android (50.9 per cent) followed by Apple's iOS (23.8 per cent) and Nokia's Symbian (11.7 per cent).[2]

The financial crisis also created problems in the industry. Commencing in 2007 in the US housing sector and financial industry and drastically worsening in September 2008, when Lehmann Brothers collapsed, the crisis then spread to the real economy causing an almost worldwide recession. Sales of mobile phones were adversely affected, especially in the West where consumer confidence plummeted. In Denmark the unemployment rate rose from 2 per cent in the summer of 2008 to 6.5 per cent in January 2010, while gross domestic product (GDP) growth was

–1.1 per cent in 2008 and –5.9 per cent in 2009 (the worst recession in the Danish economy since the Second World War).

Focusing on rather traditional mobile phone technologies, Motorola in particular faced a survival challenge during this phase of disruption. This worsened during the economic crisis, which created a rather unfriendly business environment. This is illustrated in more detail in the next section.

7.2.3   Closure of Motorola in the Cluster

Motorola had entered the cluster in 1999 by acquiring a local firm called Digianswer. In 2006, it acquired the activities of BenQ in the cluster, which had taken over Siemens' activities there in 2005. It also acquired TTP Com's subsidiary in the cluster, which had been founded by former Siemens' employees and operated as a supplier to Motorola. Motorola's Aalborg division focused on development of new mobile telephones and preparation of the production (initiating ramp-up production and finding production partners). As a result of the severe trouble in which Motorola found itself, the company headquarters decided to restructure the division, shift to the Android platform and reduce the number of newly developed models. Then it decided to move out of the European mobile market altogether, and Motorola in Aalborg was closed down.

The closure of Motorola in Aalborg was announced in November 2008, its 275 employees laid off in mid-December and the company officially wound up at the end of March 2009. At first the local management contacted Invest in Denmark and made a list of potential companies that might be able to take over the operation. Then it started to contact these companies by formal and informal channels. The formal assignment was to recoup the fixed capital (selling the equipment, buildings and so on), but the management also worked on a strategy to help the employees find employment or start new firms if the continuation of the company as a whole was to fail.

The management organized a seminar with 34 local and national firms to help the employees back to work. It also held an idea generation seminar and invited entrepreneurs and local entrepreneurship organizations to explain various ways to start a new company. The seminar generated many good ideas for new firms and also created connections between the former employees and the invited companies. The employees received up to six months full salary when they were laid off. Despite the troubled economic situation, 24 per cent of the employees had found a new job by February 2009, a share that had risen to 40 per cent by June and 52 per cent by August. And former Motorola employees also founded several new companies.

7.2.4 KIE by Former Motorola Employees

During the period 2008–10, 20 new companies were founded by ex-Motorola employees, and two parent spinoffs were also attracted to the region. Regarding the latter, the US-based company Molex founded a subsidiary by taking on a group of employees with special competencies in antenna technology. The head of the antenna unit at Motorola Aalborg started in November 2008 to look for a firm to take over their group if a takeover of the division failed. He had worked for many years in building the group of employees with unique antenna competencies and acquiring equipment. Making use of their network, they ended up contacting Molex, with whom they had worked previously as a supplier. As a result, Molex took on seven employees, acquired the specialized equipment and rented office space in the old Motorola building. Today they develop, design and test antenna solutions and have a joint project with Aalborg University on 4G LTE antennas. This type of entrepreneurship has an established history in the cluster, where several parent spinoffs have been founded by local engineers. Mobility in teams is also a frequent phenomenon when companies close down since employers look to take on well-functioning units. The Finnish company Ixonos also founded a parent spinoff at the NOVI Science Park in Aalborg, employing some of the former Motorola employees working on Android solutions.

Compared to Motorola, the two new parent spinoffs are more specialized, focusing on certain (antenna and software) functions of mobile phones. Moreover, both companies are engaged in developing technological competences in rather new systems such as 4G and the Android operating system. Therefore, we can conclude that not only did the KIE in the form of parent spinoffs (subsidiaries) secure the continuation of the existing competences stemming from Motorola, but more importantly, the influx of new competences from the parent firms advanced the further development of existing competences towards the new, now dominant mobile communications systems.

Regarding the 20 new companies, these employed a total of 44 employees including the founders. Seven of the start-ups can be labelled as hobby start-ups since the founder has a regular job in another firm. Most of the companies are based on the entrepreneurs' pre-entry experiences. However, only four can be characterized as spinoffs in the cluster following a narrow definition of the cluster, that is, including only firms dealing with wireless communications technologies. Many of them used their competencies in software development gained at Motorola to establish companies in the broader information and communications technology (ICT) sector (Table 7.1). These mostly work on developing software for other companies as IT consultants. For example, PCB-Support was founded by printed circuit board (PCB) designers working on PCB design, while Code Craft was founded by software engineers developing software for a broad range of customers.

Other firms established after the Motorola closure also show how entrepreneurs' knowledge and experience gained in former job functions at the defunct operation may be transferred to new firms. A technician, a senior design engineer and a metrology engineer founded a company called 3D-CT, which specializes in computer technology (CT) measuring. While working in Motorola, they were the first to be introduced to CT technology in the mobile industry and in Denmark. When Motorola closed down, they bought the CT scanners from the company and started providing consultancy services. The former director of the division established a management consulting firm specializing in helping firms through the liquidation process. He continues to draw on his experience of managing rounds of layoffs and the process to final close-down, including the organization of job-searching seminars for the laid-off employees.

All the spinoffs created from Motorola's exit are presented in Table 7.1. As most of the firms were created outside the wireless cluster, this illustrates that there has been knowledge dissemination from the wireless communications industry to other adjacent industries through KIE. Furthermore, a high correlation between the former position in Motorola and the new ventures indicates that the competences gained in Motorola are highly utilized in the new firms, which demonstrates transferability of the competences to other industries.

7.2.5 How an Entrepreneurial Spinoff is Born from an Existing Company: The Story of Huge Lawn Software

In this section, the entrepreneurial process of one specific spinoff company, Huge Lawn Software, will be described in detail to show how the founder developed a business idea from his experiences in an existing firm and how firm closure provided a good opportunity to start up a venture. Describing the detailed process of venture creation, this story highlights knowledge dissemination through KIE, showing that knowledge from an incumbent is kept and further developed in the cluster in spite of firm closure.

Table 7.1 Spinoffs by former Motorola employees

Firm name (founding year, exit year)	Industry	Jobs	Founder's prior position(s) at Motorola	Field of activity
3D-CT (2009)	Other	7	Technician, senior design engineer, metrology engineer	Measurement centre with CT scanner
Arcane Labs (2009)[a]	ICT	2	Software engineer, team leader, system engineer	X-box games, Classicard games
Cloud Circus (2010)	ICT	5	System engineer	Software development
Code Craft Aps (2008)	ICT	3	System engineer	Software development
Createitreal (2009)	ICT	1	Project leader engineering	Developing 3D printing and automated fabrication technologies
Flexmanagement (2010)	Other	1	Director	Management consulting
Full circle design.dk (2009, 2010)	ICT	1	Product manager	Embedded UIs, documentation of UI design
Huge Lawn Software (2009)	Wireless	5	Quality manager	iPhone and iPad applications
MVC-data (2008)	Wireless	2	Senior software engineer	SW and HW development, solutions with Bluetooth technology
NeoGrid Technologies (2010)	ICT	3	Line manager, function manager	Solutions for controlling electricity demand
NordicRefurb (2009)[a]	Other	1	Department manager	Electronic test and manufacturing equipment.
North Development consult (2009, 2009)	ICT	1	Senior electrical engineer	Engineering consulting
OR Pro (2009)[a]	Other	1	Requirement manager	Project management

Firm name (founding year, exit year)	Industry	Jobs	Founder's prior position(s) at Motorola	Field of activity
PartDesign (2009)	Other	2	Sourcing manager, mechanical project leader	Mechanic construction, FEM analysis, sourcing in China
PCB-support (2009)	ICT	2	PCB designer	PCB design
Proint s.m.b.a. (2009)[a]	ICT	2	Project leader, programme manager	IT consulting
SES IT (2010, 2010)	ICT	1	Software test engineer	IT consultant
Synergile (2008)[a]	Wireless	1	Engineering lead	RF eEngineering solutions
Unpaq (2009)[a]	Wireless	1	Software engineer	Software, Mac OSX, iPhone
Utopia Solutions (2009)[a]	ICT	2	Software engineer	Web shops and custom web-solutions

Note: [a] Hobby start-ups: the founders have regular jobs in another company. HW: Hardware; RF: Radio frequency; SW: Software; UI: User interface.

Uffe Koch, the founder of Huge Lawn Software, has an engineering education with specialization in IT and computer technology. He was working in British TTPCom's local subsidiary when Motorola acquired the firm, in 2004. TTPCom developed mobile phones and software for other firms and Motorola was one of their biggest customers. When the firm was acquired by Motorola, Koch had high hopes of the opportunities that Motorola would bring as one of the major companies in the industry. However, the software that he and his colleagues had worked on for many years was given a low priority compared to the other projects already running in Motorola and in the end the project was completely curtailed. It was about then that he realized the potential of iPhones (smartphones). He tried to convince Motorola that the company needed to pay more attention to the new technologies for smartphones, but he did not succeed.

When his ideas were not accepted in Motorola, Koch started to think about establishing his own company, to develop applications and other small programs for smartphones. He started investigating how to start up a business and took a (weekly) course in entrepreneurship. In this way, he was taking the first step towards starting his own business while he was still employed at Motorola. When the news on the closure of Motorola came in 2008, he had already decided to quit his job and had written a letter of resignation. However, it turned out that, due to his seniority in the company, he could get a half year's full salary from the time of closure. He decided to utilize this opportunity to realize the idea of establishing his own company. Since he had been developing the idea and had prepared for the opportunity, he was able to start as self-employed from the day he lost his job at Motorola.

The local entrepreneurship organization offered 12 hours of consulting for a good price and Koch took the offer to bring the idea into practice. Although he had experience in developing applications and software for a different operating system, he decided to enter the market for iPhone applications as he found the Apple development tools and environment exciting and saw huge business opportunities in this market. He knew that he had the relevant knowledge, experience and not least network to make this work. In the starting phase, Huge Lawn Software was mostly hired to develop applications for large company and organization marketing. These apps were distributed free to customers and other stakeholders, and Huge Lawn Software was paid for the development work directly by its customers. However, in some cases, some applications developed for marketing purposes were found to be unique and so useful that they were sold in Apple's app store and even became very popular as a category in their own right. The company grew quite quickly and three in-house developers and various freelancers were hired. Since its foundation, this company has developed, among others, an interactive application for a major Danish radio station, a weather forecasting application for a windmill company and an application for a campaign that the National Board of Health is running. In 2012, it announced that it now is also capable of developing Android apps.

7.3 WHAT HAVE WE LEARNED?

This section answers the questions posed in the introduction.

> How do the existing firms and knowledge base affect future KIE?
>
> To what extent does knowledge diffusion take place through KIE from exiting firms?
>
> How did the entrepreneurs' pre-entry experiences influence their new venture?

What effect does KIE from firm exit in one industry have on other industries in the region?

The case study in this chapter describes KIE in the form of spinoff activities in the wireless cluster in a region of Northern Denmark. To start with, the history of the cluster shows that firms that were successful in a certain industry have created spinoffs of many generations that diversified into related fields. The KIE was indeed the driving force behind the formation of the cluster, and this demonstrates how existing firms and the knowledge base affect future KIE.

Moving on to the focus of the case study, namely the KIE from the exit of Motorola in the cluster in 2009, a similar pattern of spinoff activities is observed. The spinoff pattern shows that the knowledge and the experience gained by the founders in the former workplace contributed positively to new venture creation. Firstly, most founders established new firms in either the same wireless communications industry or the related ICT industry. As most of the employees in Motorola were R&D engineers, the technological competences that they possess were transferred to the new company, which is clearly shown in their choice of industry. It is also apparent that there is a connection between the former job functions in Motorola and the services and products that the new firms provide. Most of the spinoffs are consulting firms that offer services that fall within their competences utilized in their old jobs. Software developers and hardware developers founded consulting firms that offer consulting within software development and hardware development, respectively; a technician who used to work with CT on the measurement of industrial products took over the equipment from Motorola and started a company measuring diverse industrial products for customers.

Moreover, the knowledge the founders accumulated on the market and the industry also helped them detect good business opportunities. In the case of Huge Lawn Software, the founder spotted a lucrative business opportunity in the iPhone app market because he was engaged in developing software in one of the biggest mobile phone producers in the industry. He knew exactly how the industry and the technologies were developing in this field. Not only did he have the skills to try out Apple's development tools, but he also had enough knowledge of the market to analyse the business potential of the idea. All this goes to show that existing firms and their knowledge base can strongly affect the future KIE in a region and that the entrepreneur's pre-entry experiences influence the creation of new ventures.

The knowledge diffusion in this case took place through the mobility of the employees released through the Motorola firm closure. To find out to what extent the knowledge diffusion took place through KIE, it is necessary to take a look at how many of the 275 former Motorola employees found a new job in existing companies and how many participated in KIE through spinoff activities. Out of 247 employees that had found employment as of 2011, 220 people were working in existing companies and 27 had founded new ventures. This means that about 10 per cent of the released workforce from the existing company contributed to the knowledge diffusion by KIE. Thus most diffusion of knowledge would seem to have taken place through the mobility of employees who simply got new jobs. The share of KIE appears to be high given the unfriendly business environment during the financial crisis, but it is uncertain if many of these will survive or grow substantially in the future.

We have also learned that firm exit in one industry has an effect on KIE in other industries in the region. The closure of Motorola created spinoffs, the majority of which were in industries other than that of wireless communications. Only four out of 20 new firms were established within the boundary of the wireless communications cluster. A total of 11 companies can be identified as operating within the broader boundary of the ICT industry, while five firms moved into totally different areas. As many founders utilize their specialized competences in their start-ups, we can assume that the ICT and other unrelated industries will benefit from the knowledge these new firms bring. Thus, knowledge diffusion does take place through KIE from existing firms, but it appears that, in this case of a declining cluster, most KIEs start up in related industries. This is because a declining cluster and the very turbulent mobile phone industry do not favour the entry of small start-ups. However, the KIE from Motorola are to a large extent still based on the existing knowledge base from Motorola.

7.4 QUESTIONS FOR FURTHER REFLECTION

Explain how the closure of Motorola leads to KIE.

Discuss the extent to which entrepreneurs create their new ventures based on previous work experiences.

How do you think the previous experience of the founder will affect the performance of the new venture in comparison with other start-ups without pre-entry experience?

Discuss the importance of knowledge diffusion through spinoff activities in the context of other industries (for example, in low-tech industries).

Discuss positive and negative effects of firm closure in a regional economy.

Discuss the future of the Motorola spinoffs in relation to the development of the mobile communications industry worldwide.

NOTES

1. Since the case study keeps track of a large number of firms in the cluster and the KIE described should be understood in the context of the development of the specific industry and the region, the chapter will not apply anonymity like the rest of the chapters in the book.
2. Numbers from Gartner reports on *Market Share: Mobile Devices by Region and Country*, available at http://www.gartner.com (accessed 31 May 2012).

REFERENCES

Buenstorf, G. and S. Klepper (2009), 'Heritage and agglomeration: the Akron tyre cluster revisited', *Economic Journal*, **119** (537), 705–33.
Christensen, C. (1997), *The Innovator's Dilemma*, Boston, MA: Harvard Business School Press.
Dahl, M.S. and T. Reichstein (2007), 'Are you experienced? Prior experience and the survival of new organizations', *Industry and Innovation*, **14** (5), 497–511.
Dahl, M.S. and O. Sorenson (2012), 'Home sweet home: entrepreneurs' location choices and the performance of their ventures', *Management Science, Articles in Advance*, **58** (6), 1059–71.
Garnsey, E. and P. Heffernan (2005), 'High-technology clustering through spin-out and attraction: the Cambridge case', *Regional Studies*, **39** (8), 1127–44.
Klepper, S. (2010), 'The origin and growth of industry clusters: the making of Silicon Valley and Detroit', *Journal of Urban Economics*, **67** (1), 15–32.
Utterback, J.M. (1994), *Mastering the Dynamics of Innovation*, Boston, MA: Harvard Business School Press.

8. Entrepreneurial exploitation of creative destruction and the ambiguity of knowledge in the emerging field of digital advertising

Oskar Broberg, Ann-Sofie Axelsson and Gustav Sjöblom

8.1 INTRODUCTION

This chapter addresses how knowledge intensive entrepreneurship (KIE) in professional service firms is affected by the fact that knowledge is an uncertain asset. What this means is that in the analysis of KIE it is often impossible to separate knowledge and analytical skills from flexibility, organizing capacities, social skills and rhetorical capabilities in constructing an image of expertise. This uncertainty is further aggravated by the fact that the output – be it audit reports or advertising campaigns – tends to be difficult to evaluate objectively for outsiders. Also, the contributions of the client and the consultant are hard to disentangle. Although it is clear that specific skills – such as technical expertise, market understanding and business knowledge – are the foundation of entrepreneurial ventures, it is often difficult to clearly define and value this knowledge. In this chapter we use the concept of 'ambiguity of knowledge' to pinpoint this uncertainty and to analyse its effect on KIE in digital advertising (Robertson and Swan, 2003; Alvesson, 2004).

In this chapter we follow two entrepreneurs, co-founders of a digital advertising agency in a small European country, during two turbulent decades. We look at how the two entrepreneurs, in their actions and interactions during their careers, seized the opportunities created during this period and handled the ambiguity of knowledge in order to create successful KIE ventures. These two individuals are part of a larger sample of 20 entrepreneurs we have studied to see how advertising agencies have adopted the Internet and to find out the role of award shows in their entrepreneurial success.

In order to better understand the case study in this chapter, we need to know a bit more about its main business activities. A typical assignment for a digital agency is to create a website or an Internet-based campaign for a client, a specific brand, in order to direct the public's attention to this brand and increase its sales figures in the short run and its popularity in the long run. After the campaign is over or the website has been launched, the digital agency can take part in award shows, such as the Cannes Lions International Festival of Creativity, in competition with other agencies, for awards for the best campaign or website. Award shows are considered very important by many actors in the business, especially among the leading circles of internationally active agencies. This is also true for many global clients, since it is clearly communicated through the jury judgements what good advertising is and which advertising agencies are the best. However, the judgement is rather subjective since it is made by juries consisting of professionals from within the field. It is also often difficult to ascribe the knowledge to one specific actor since the products (the digital campaigns, the websites) are usually co-produced by the client and the digital agency.

Knowledge ambiguity can also be observed in other parts of the digital advertising business. The technological knowledge consists of hard programming skills, but also creative and more indefinable talents such as art direction. The market knowledge rests to a large extent on intuition of how artistic representations of brands in digital channels, particularly on the Internet, are perceived. The business knowledge consists to a high degree of managing the corporate image, employee identities and social relations. The knowledge required is thus, across the board, of a rather intuitive and relational nature – knowledge is something that people do and which is constructed and negotiated through social interaction (Newell et al., 2009). Therefore, KIE in digital advertising cannot be described as the application of a set of mere functional or instrumental resources. It is rather about managing fluid and ambiguous resources.

Since our case study is heavily dependent on the development and application of the Internet, it is important to highlight another crucial circumstance of this case: 'creative destruction'. The notion of creative destruction refers to the way times of rapid technological and institutional change create opportunities for the formation of new combinations of knowledge and other resources into new entrepreneurial ventures (Schumpeter, 1942). Creative destruction may be regarded as a generic phenomenon of capitalism, which means that it is essentially a permanent condition, but its consequences are especially salient in the wake of radical innovations, such as, in our case, the Internet (McKnight et al., 2001; Hjorth and Steyaert, 2003). However, creative destruction does not only open up new opportunities and markets but also closes doors and destroys old markets. These two conditions, creative destruction and ambiguity of knowledge, create opportunities for the entrepreneurs in this specific field of KIE business.

Following Alvesson, who argues that successful KIE depends on the management of rhetoric, image and social processes, we suggest that the entrepreneurs solidify ambiguous knowledge in order to build up and sustain a position in their field of business (Alvesson, 2001, 2004). This is done (1) inwards (within the individual or the firm) by creating an identity of being knowledgeable, with the help of rhetoric; (2) outwards (towards competitors and clients) by being knowledgeable, through images of the individual or firm; and (3) with the help of relationships with important actors who may make the individual or firm appear knowledgeable.

Summing up this introduction, the chapter is guided by two questions that take their starting point in the above-described framework:

> What kind of entrepreneurial opportunities were created during the breakthrough of the Internet in regard to the advertising business?

> How did the entrepreneurs studied here seize these opportunities in order to build up and sustain their position in this knowledge intensive business?

8.2 CASE STUDY: DIGITAL ADVERTISING

The availability of the Internet and other digital marketing channels has contributed to a radical change in the advertising business over the last 10 to 15 years. In the European country in question here, the development of digital advertising was driven by small entrepreneurial startups rather than by the incumbent firms in traditional advertising. The entrepreneurial act that we study is based on opportunities that arose around the turn of the millennium, when the Internet partly undermined old business models and eroded the boundaries between advertising, IT, media and management consulting.

This structural transformation can be understood as a creative destruction process set in motion by technological innovation (for example, Internet protocols, web browsers) and institutional innovation (deregulation). The innovation of the Internet – or rather the expectations of it –

created new professional jurisdictions that had to be exploited with new combinations of skills. In this context, the key knowledge often turned out to be skills that had not previously been perceived as useful knowledge. For example, at a time when users were overwhelmed with information, the ability to draw attention to a website through humorous content proved to be a valuable asset. Digital advertising came into being through entrepreneurs and creative individuals with little previous experience of advertising. Over the course of the following decade, the incumbent advertising firms gradually caught up and closed the entrepreneurial window, creating new challenges for the entrepreneurial start-ups.

In the following, we trace the professional history of two entrepreneurs – hereafter referred to as Mathew and Nicholas – from the early 1990s up until 2010. Mathew and Nicholas both began their professional trajectories in the digital advertising field in the early 1990s by taking part in various Internet-related projects but did not set up an agency of their own until 2000 – immediately acquiring global acclaim for their creativity. We describe, in particular, how their entrepreneurship in the field of digital advertising was shaped by two circumstances – an ongoing process of creative destruction in the surrounding environment and pursuing strategies to solidify the ambiguous knowledge involved.

8.2.1 The Creation of a New Media Landscape

In the late 1980s and early 1990s, many European countries deregulated different sectors of their media markets. As part of a bigger process of market liberalization, the monopolies of government-run telephone and broadcasting companies were challenged. In the country in question here, the two state-run television channels were complemented by a third – commercially financed – channel. This opened up new possibilities for the advertising industry and, in just a few years, television was the second largest source of revenue for the advertising business. One entrepreneurial challenger, in particular, here called Media Phase, saw the opportunities created by this liberalization. During the 1980s and 1990s, this firm started a telephone company, television channels, magazines and several companies in digital media. With a solid forest company at the bottom of its portfolio and a determined executive at the top, the company had both the financial muscle and visions needed for its expansionary strategy. Beside this institutional change, the early 1990s was also the time when personal computers (PCs) made their way into people's homes. Hence, the combination of institutional change and digital dawn set off a process of creative destruction with old and new media companies fighting to establish themselves in a new media landscape.

Our point of entry is 1994, when the government-run telephone and postal companies launched big digital projects (web portals) at the same time as Media Phase launched a subsidiary company aimed at developing more content-oriented digital business concepts.

At this stage, there was no such thing as digital advertising. However, there was the first generation (mostly young men) that had grown up with computers and become self-taught digital creatives who knew far more about multi-media, programming and animation than the established media professionals at the time. It was, however, still unclear whether their playing and programming would make any difference to their professional careers. By the mid-1990s, this generation was in their early twenties and in a transitional stage between education and work. One of these young men was Nicholas. Though no programmer, he had an interest in the intersection between technology and creativity:

> I am not particularly good at organic art, drawing by hand and what have you. But I have always liked communication and advertising and TV graphics. When I was young I recorded vignettes from MTV and Eurosport, just to watch how they moved. I thought it was awesome.

This rather nerdy interest in technologically designed popular culture would turn out to be economically valuable, as it became the foundation for his digital design skills. In 1994, having just finished art school in the UK, Nicholas was back home again, applying for jobs, and he started to work for a traditional advertising agency. In 1996, his girlfriend (working at one of the above-mentioned web portals) told him about a design competition. The task was to promote the portal by building a website, and the prize was a Gateway 2000 PC. He designed the site but let a friend do the programming. This was the first time he had ever designed a website and he won first prize – which placed him on the map of knowledgeable web designers.

Mathew's entry into the digital arena, on the other hand, was a result of his years as a freelancing company lawyer, during which time he developed his entrepreneurial skills in various media-related projects. In one of these ventures, he was approached by the above-mentioned Media Phase and he started working for the company. The job situated him at the centre of events in the mid-1990s, as he worked with new business models, new media channels and, not least, new media content.

Hence, the two would-be entrepreneurs entered the digital business from different angles, neither of them particularly knowledgeable in technical specificities. On the contrary, they soon learned that a professional identity could be built around the way their respective competencies in design and business could be deployed in a digital environment. Furthermore, social relations proved important to both of them, because they provided them with job opportunities as well as new influence.

8.2.2 Lobster Delivery as a Means to Prove Digital Competence

In 1996, the expansion of the Internet was picking up speed, and digital companies were popping up everywhere – most of them building websites or venturing into the virgin field of CD-Rom production. Expectations of digital business were rising and, by 1999, the boom had turned into an outright bubble. Many companies experienced internal conflicts when venture capitalists demanded quantity rather than quality and expansionary plans rather than consolidated strategies. The primary aim of these operations was to buy up digital companies and float them as quickly as possible. Logically, the frustration among the employees rose as these operations escalated in numbers and sheer size. The economic climate showed that digital business had plenty of opportunities, and it was a formative process for many of the actors in the field.

During the boom, a first generation of digital agencies with an advertising edge was established. The businesses were usually small startups and the life cycles of these firms were very short: within a few years they had either been bought up and/or gone bankrupt. The story of Nicholas and Mathew illustrates the forces at play. In the wake of the website competition, Nicholas received job offers from various companies. Since digital advertising, at the time, was a field under construction with great uncertainties regarding what the field could be and what was good digital advertising, this first competition clearly helped create an image of him as knowledgeable in the field.

Despite the many possibilities offered to him, he decided to go with the offer made to him by the company he was already working for, as it set up a digital agency and made him a partner. A brother-in-law of the founder of the digital agency, Mathew was also offered a job and partnership. Mathew's most important contribution to the venture can be said to have been an extensive social network and a curious attitude towards the potential of the new media. The company was set up with a clear digital focus, though it was still unclear what Internet advertising would really mean, and the clients knew even less of what could be expected from a digital campaign.

Nevertheless, in 1997 the most prestigious national advertising award show added 'Internet' as a competition category, though no prize was awarded since the jury did not regard any of the contributions good enough. The year after, however, Mathew was awarded first prize as project leader for a web campaign for the national post office. An ordinary letter – a direct mail – was sent out to a couple of hundred persons of power (in economic and social terms) with a request that they log on to the web shop set up for the campaign. There they could choose from a number of products (among them a freshly boiled lobster) to order. Within a couple of hours, to many people's surprise, the product (most often a lobster) was delivered to the door.

The campaign was, in many senses, a key event during this phase of creative destruction. First, the campaign gave a specially targeted number of powerful people an introductory glimpse of what the Internet could be or become – a virtual link between real actors. Spreading their picture of the Internet to key actors at this early stage was a strategic and important entrepreneurial step towards future collaborations, assignments and successes. Second, the campaign showed hesitant traditional advertising agencies the meaning of and value in the Internet as a commercial medium. Apart from providing an efficient service, the website created brand engagement spiked with a sense of humour – a characteristic of digital advertising ever since. Other digital agencies also realized how digital campaigns could be designed. Third, by winning the new Internet category, they showed potential customers that they could successfully make use of the new medium. It is obvious that the award-winning itself was, in many ways, more important than the campaign. Whereas the campaign gave the national post office attention, it was the advertising companies that benefited most, not least in the long run. The award and the attention that followed, from competitors as well as potential clients, became in Alvesson's terminology an important part of the image created of the agency and its creative directors as knowledgeable and cool (Alvesson, 2004). The jury described the winning campaign as 'a brilliant collaboration between two worlds: the real reality and the virtual reality'. Hence, the knowledge exploited was combined visionary thinking in design and business rather than excellence in technical skills.

Given the state of the market in 1998, it was more or less inevitable that venture capitalists would circle around the award-winning agency. The quickly achieved image of success translated into economic value, and the majority owners could not resist one of the offers. They sold it in secrecy in 1999 and expansion became the first priority with the new owners, at the expense of crafting visionary campaigns. Nicholas and Mathew found themselves in a company with two outside investors they disliked from the first meeting. A debt-driven expansion took off in which more and more people were employed with less and less relevant experience. The situation quickly became untenable, and the following winter Mathew and Nicholas left the company. In 2001 the company, drained of its main creative powers, filed for bankruptcy.

8.2.3   Setting up One's Own Shop

The puncture of the dot.com bubble in 2001 resulted in a peculiar entrepreneurial landscape. On the one hand, investors disappeared and there was a heated public debate on how blind faith in technology had shaped the previous years. There seemed to be a digital backlash. On the other hand, the radical innovation itself – widespread use of the Internet – continued to spread right through the crisis. In particular, we can see how technological innovations such as Flash technology and increased bandwidth made more elaborate digital campaigns accessible to large audiences. From 1998 onwards, we can also see that the revenues of Internet advertising soared, surpassing the categories 'radio' and 'out-door' in 2000 and continuing to rise during the first years of the new decade.

The result of this development was a number of new startups in 2000 to 2003, with founders having the experiences of the dot.com fresh in their memories. As one entrepreneur in our larger sample explained in an interview:

> It felt like it was time to set up one's own shop, because I felt I had been tricked to follows others' visions.

There was a feeling among several of these entrepreneurs that their competencies had not been fully appreciated. Traditional agencies were happy to use digital agencies as production companies but they were unwilling to share the glory when campaigns were acknowledged and awarded. The digital advertisers at the time both collaborated and competed with traditional advertisers but had a very different experience of and view on the Internet, something that seems to have given the digital entrepreneurs a specific identity. This identity and feeling of otherness in relation to traditional advertisers made the digital advertisers form an informal national network. As Mathew explained, the identity rested on a view that the Internet was not just another channel in the media landscape but a universe of its own. Hence, the advertisers, he said, had to rethink how corporate images were constructed in the digital age, as well as how social relations were formed and sustained. Not all digital advertisers were this outspoken, but Mathew's views on the matter are of importance, as he quickly became an informal spokesperson for this group of digital advertisers.

After leaving the venture capitalists behind, Mathew convinced Nicholas and two other colleagues to start up a new agency – here called Grandmother – and this company soon became the leading digital agency of this informal network. Their vision was clear from the beginning: the business should rest on their knowledge of how to create world-class digital advertising. Nobody could, of course, say exactly what that was, but they were confident of their skills. Events would soon prove them right and the most important leverage on this knowledge came from international award shows.

One of Grandmother's first clients was a dairy company. The campaign was outsourced to them from a traditional advertising agency, where Internet campaigns were considered less important than traditional ones (newspaper, TV). With a minimal budget and simple means, they created The Music Machine, an interactive website where the visitor could manipulate a dancing and singing cow. The mix of doll play and pop music – all programmed in Shockwave – was technically speaking low-tech. However, the format was absolute high-tech and the campaign spread around the world as one of the first viral campaigns. The campaign won a number of advertising awards in 2001, primarily the most prestigious Grand Prix at the Cannes Lions International Festival of Creativity. There and then, Grandmother was out on the international market. The campaign strengthened the image of Grandmother as an agency that managed to combine the opportunities of digital media with a feeling for elements of popular culture that could be used to attract the attention of an Internet audience. A concrete result of this was that the award led to a number of new clients. Another result was that Mathew and Nicholas were invited to become jury members of the Cannes Festival Clio Awards and Eurobest. Participation in juries became an outspoken strategy of the company. Jury work was a way to develop important social relations within the field. It gave status to be invited and was also a practical way of keeping up to date with advertising trends from all over the world.

8.2.4 Managing Success

The generation of digital advertising firms established in the wake of the dot.com bubble did well due to a combination of a growing business in general and creative success. The network of digital advertisers and agencies was strengthened, as the social relations were sustained through friendly competition and knowledge-sharing at events like award shows and Creative Social, an informal network of advertisers. Tellingly, Mathew labelled his competitors 'soulmates'. This national network of friendly competitors and their identities was also strengthened by the fact that the digital agencies, including Grandmother, did not, at the time, belong to any larger corporate network, which was often the case abroad. The lack of a corporate hierarchy gave the agencies and their creative directors a sense of independence and a true feeling of being in control of their own capacities. If and when their campaigns were acknowledged, they knew it was due to their own knowledge.

In the coming years, when these firms, year after year, climbed in the international creativity rankings, the field-specific knowledge turned out to be economically valuable. In the first years, Grandmother experienced an organic growth phase, the number of employees rose from 10 to 20 and the turnover per employee approached the average for a traditional advertising agency. The firm also attracted the attention of international media companies, leaving the owners with the question of how to handle the success – develop the firm further or sell it? In a knowledge intensive service industry, this is particularly problematic since the human capital represents the lion's share of the brand value. This means that the firm is worth little without its staff. Furthermore, given the ambiguity of knowledge, the human capital is in itself difficult to assess.

Once again, the case of Grandmother illustrates this. In late 2002, the agency was offered, and accepted, the digital account of a global mobile telephone company. The resulting campaigns received awards nationally and internationally, and the appetite for international expansion grew. When, in 2005, a British media network made a good offer for Grandmother to become part of its global digital network, the owners considered the timing to be right. They sold their shares, but with the idea that they would continue to develop the company. However, the hopes of fruitful cooperation were dashed in 2007 when it was closing a deal with a big multinational client. The plan was that Grandmother would open an agency in New York in order to be closer to its big client, but, instead, the media network handed over the contract to already established agencies in the USA. The distrust grew even further when the mobile telephone company account, against Grandmother's will, was taken over by other digital agencies within the network. The end was near for Grandmother. In November 2009, Nicholas had had enough and accepted an offer and left for a New York-based agency and, only a few months later, Mathew also decided to leave. Within a few weeks, ten more people left Grandmother, and in April 2010 the owners decided to close down the agency for good.

Ironically, the success continued after the shutdown, as Grandmother won its sixth Lion in Cannes for its last cooperation with the mobile phone company. The Music Machine had brought them into the international market, but it was the mobile phone company that supplied the resources needed to act on a big scale. The company became the most important client because of its long-term trust in the inventive power and worldwide influence of the agency's creative directors. The step from the freshly boiled lobster in 1997 to the real-time display of people's text messages on huge signs in 2009 is in fact not very big. One could say that they stood by their creative ideas, but realizing them on a bigger scale as the successful management of the ambiguous knowledge released the necessary financial resources. The strategy to target international advertising award shows proved ingenious. This became the key in terms of image, identity and social relations. The final Lion, received after Grandmother had been closed down, signifies the massive strength of the image created during the agency's lifetime.

8.3   WHAT HAVE WE LEARNED?

This chapter was guided by two questions:

> What kind of entrepreneurial opportunities were created during the breakthrough of the Internet in regard to the advertising business?

> How did the entrepreneurs studied here seize these opportunities in order to build up and sustain their position in this knowledge intensive business?

These questions are answered in the following by revisiting the entrepreneurial story that we have told, bringing up the most significant episodes. During the period from the early 1990s up until 2010, the field of digital advertising was characterized by three conditions: market growth, technological shifts and the ambiguity of knowledge. All of these have continuously opened up entrepreneurial opportunities, and it is therefore natural that a significant process of creative destruction can be identified. Companies have been started and shut down, successful startups have been taken over by incumbent firms and creative individuals from awarded startups have been actively headhunted by large international companies. In short, managing these three conditions has been a prerequisite of a successful entrepreneurial venture. Following the professional trajectory of Mathew and Nicholas, the creative destruction process in this chapter can be thought of as divided into four subsequent phases characterized by changes in the existing market conditions and the creation of specific entrepreneurial opportunities.

During the first phase, which was characterized by the deregulation of the media market, Mathew and Nicholas established themselves in the digital arena. Coming from different backgrounds – law and art – they explored how their knowledge could be deployed in the new media landscape.

The second phase was characterized by the breakthrough of the Internet and the way the possibility of distributing advertisements digitally opened up new entrepreneurial opportunities. Mathew and Nicholas developed their identity and image as knowledgeable in this new media landscape in which IT and advertising were the big landmarks, which resulted in offers to join entrepreneurial ventures initiated by people around them.

The third phase was the post-dot.com vacuum, when Mathew and Nicholas left their employer to establish their own digital agency, Grandmother. The startup was a reaction to venture capitalists' attempt to brutally drive the business from creativity to capital, but also a way forward to increased creative independence. During this period, Mathew and Nicholas made use of the knowledge they had picked up early in their careers – technical expertise, market understanding and business knowledge – and transformed it into digital advertising campaigns and websites. They also put much effort into building the firm's international image and social network by taking part in international award shows as contestants and jury members.

The fourth phase was characterized by the fact that incumbent firms were catching up. Thanks to Grandmother's successful participation in international award shows, international players wanted the agency to become integrated in their corporate networks. The creative agency that could make people in power order lobsters online on demand was wanted as a part of the networks' businesses, but obviously more as an ornament of coolness for the network than as an actor acting on its own premises. Speaking in Alvesson's terms, Grandmother became a part of the corporate network's own image building in order to solidify their knowledge ambiguity.

Digital advertising is characterized by the ambiguity of knowledge and has therefore been an ideal field for multi-talented actors. The actors combined knowledge from different fields and transformed it into practice, making websites or interactive campaigns. Since the digital advertising field was immature at the time, their fast and decisive actions established a precedent for what could and should be done in terms of digital advertising campaigns. Thereby, the entrepreneurial potential was also related to a process of co-creation of the field. Actors that succeeded in terms of building identity, image and social relations were also co-creators of the field in question. These positive feedback loops were reinforced by the international award shows. Grandmother took the decision early on to strategically target international award shows. The agency identified that the award shows were the hubs of the ambiguous digital landscape, where it could establish its image towards customers as well as competitors (and venture capitalists), its self-identity and create its important social relations. This strategic decision was crucial since the quality of the work (and the excellence of the agency) could almost not be measured in any other way than through the peer-reviewing process of the award show. However, creating success is one thing and sustaining it is something else. When the success, both at home and abroad, was a fact and international customers and media companies started to show interest, the owners of Grandmother decided that selling the firm to a bigger player – but keeping the creative control – was the next step to take on the entrepreneurial ladder. What they may not have realized was that the buyer had an agenda of its own in how to manage the knowledge ambiguity of the advertising sector. To acquire the cool and successful Grandmother was part of the network's own image creation. However, it was never in the minds of the entrepreneurs to end up as a decorative sidekick to other players. Leaving Grandmother and taking the knowledge with them was the entrepreneurs' way of saying just that. The Lion won after the new owners had put Grandmother to sleep which gave the entrepreneurs their final recognition.

8.4 QUESTIONS FOR FURTHER REFLECTION

What kind of business knowledge was critical for the entrepreneurial ventures in this case of digital advertising?

Award shows play an important role in translating knowledge into economic value. Are there similar mechanisms in other knowledge intensive industries? If no, why not? If yes, exemplify.

What was the role of venture capital in this case? Could it have been different?

What conflicts between entrepreneurial control and international business ambitions can be identified? Could these conflicts have been avoided or handled differently?

What can digital advertising agencies (or other knowledge intensive companies) of today learn from this case? In what way could this case inspire a company's strategy?

REFERENCES

Alvesson, M. (2001), 'Knowledge work: ambiguity, image and identity', *Human Relations*, **54** (7), 863–86.

Alvesson, M. (2004), *Knowledge Work and Knowledge-intensive Firms*, Oxford: Oxford University Press.

Hjorth, D. and C. Steyaert (2003), 'Entrepreneurship beyond (a new) economy: creative swarms and pathological zones', in C. Steyaert and D. Hjorth (eds), *New Movements in Entrepreneurship*, Cheltenham, UK and Northampton, MA, USA: Edward Elgar, pp. 286–310.

McKnight, L.W., P.M. Vaaler and R.L. Katz (eds) (2001), *Creative Destruction: Business Survival Strategies in the Global Internet Economy*, Cambridge, MA: MIT Press.

Newell, S., M. Robertson, H. Scarbrough and J. Swan (eds) (2009), *Managing Knowledge Work and Innovation*, Basingstoke: Palgrave.

Robertson, M. and J. Swan (2003), 'Control – what control? Culture and ambiguity within a knowledge intensive firm', *Journal of Management Studies*, **40** (4), 831–58.

Schumpeter, J.A. (1942), *Capitalism, Socialism, and Democracy*, London: Harper & Brothers.

9. Knowledge reallocation and challenges for KIE: the case of the European roller coaster industry

Bram Timmermans, Rudi Bekkers and Luca Bordoli

9.1 INTRODUCTION

When firms and individuals act on opportunities, either by starting a new venture or by diversifying the existing product portfolio through innovation, existing knowledge is reallocated and applied in new situations. This is also the case for knowledge intensive entrepreneurship (KIE), which according to the definition provided in this volume, involves the start of a new business that is innovative, has significant knowledge intensity in their activities and develops innovative opportunities in diverse sectors. It might be problematic, however, for new firms to enter due to a need for large investments or the sophistication of the knowledge that can only be handled by larger, more established firms. This may be particularly true for industries that produce complex products and where customers base their buying decision on reputation, which is in fact the case in the roller coaster industry that is the focus of this chapter.

Over the years, researchers have investigated the role of pre-entry knowledge and how the nature of this knowledge affects entry. These studies have investigated a large diversity of industries, for example, the evolution of the automobile industry, as presented in Klepper (2009) and Boschma and Wenting (2007), but also the evolution of knowledge intensive and high-tech industries like the production of lasers (Buenstorf, 2007). The interest has led to a typology of entry modes, mainly distinguishing between pre-entry knowledge and the experience of the founders alongside the relationship of the entrant with the parent firm. Helfat and Lieberman (2002) have formulated the most common distinctions, which are: diversifying entrants, parent company activity and de novo entrants. The latter category, which includes entrepreneurial spin-offs, experienced entrepreneurs and inexperienced entrepreneurs, is where the new ventures are found that are not controlled by existing firms. To identify the modes of entry, one needs to identify the background information of firms and founders.

The dominant form of entry will vary between industries. As highlighted by Boschma and Wenting (2007), in the early stage of an industry, it is most likely that diversified entry will play a more important role than any other form of entry. The argument behind this reasoning is that the number of firms with expertise in a new industry is limited and entrepreneurs will operate within the framework of an existing organization in order to utilize the larger set of (knowledge) resources that are available in existing firms. In the later stages, when the industry is more established, entrepreneurial spin-offs will occur more frequently. In some industries these spin-offs will become the dominant form of entry, for example, in the automobile industry (Klepper, 2009), while in other industries the dominant form of entry remains to be that of diversified entry, for example, the television receiver industry (Klepper and Simons, 2000).

Notwithstanding the above, it is not only the mode of entry that is of importance, but also the character of the pre-entry experience. For example, firms that possess the skills and competences in building bikes and coaches have an advantage when entering the automobile industry compared to firms that have other pre-entry skills (Boschma and Wenting, 2007). However, this relatedness can have many different dimensions.

This chapter examines the importance of pre-entry knowledge of the companies that enter the European steel roller coaster industry, and addresses how KIE emerges in this particular industry environment. A roller coaster can be classified as a complex product that requires substantial engineering competences, particularly on the large thrill rides. This complexity makes pre-entry knowledge an important factor. Inexperienced entrants may face considerable challenges to succeed in this industry. We shall distinguish the following modes of entry:

> Category A: Diversified entry, market: firms that enter an industry and where the pre-entry industry can be characterized as having experience in the same market.

> Category B: Diversified entry, technology: firms that enter an industry and where the pre-entry industry can be characterized as having experience in similar technological fields.

Category C: Parent spin-off: new ventures founded under the control of the parent firms in order to exploit the market and/or technological competences in the roller coaster industry.

Category D: Entrepreneurial spin-off: new ventures founded by entrepreneurs that leave a roller coaster manufacturer to start their own roller coaster firm.

Other forms of entry that are found in the literature, such as inexperienced entry by entrepreneurs, are virtually non-existent in this specific industry.

This chapter starts with a technological history of roller coasters. Then we discuss the various forms of entry by providing corresponding examples from Italy, Germany, Switzerland and the Netherlands. These are the main roller coaster producing countries in Europe. This case study will address the following questions:

What are the dominant modes of entry in the roller coaster industry? What is the role of KIE?

How does a particular level of pre-entry experience affect the complexity of the products of the entrant, and how does this complexity affect new venture creation?

What are the reasons for entrepreneurs to leave their parent firm and establish a new business?

How do the characteristics of the parent firm leave a trace in the characteristics of the KIE?

9.2 THE EUROPEAN STEEL ROLLER COASTER INDUSTRY

The first European steel roller coaster was introduced in 1953 in Italy; however, the origin of the roller coaster dates back centuries earlier. According to historical records, the first roller coasters were located in fifteenth-century Russia, which is still reflected by the French word for roller coasters, *montagnes russes*. Despite this long history it took several centuries more before LaMarcus Thompson in the USA designed the first commercial roller coaster in 1884. He was granted a patent for its design shortly after (Cartmell, 1987; Lanfer, 1998).

Early roller coasters were invariably built out of wood. Later, steel was gradually introduced into roller coaster manufacturing. This started with the tracks and the occasional part of the ride's supporting structure. It was not before the early 1950s when the first roller coasters were produced that were entirely made of steel. Due to the use of this material, it was no longer necessary to use massive amounts of wood and the total usage of material decreased considerably, resulting in lower production and transportation costs (Lanfer, 1998). This development helped the roller coaster out of a crisis that it had entered after the 1930s with the closure of many amusement parks (Cartmell, 1987). Despite the fact that steel soon started to dominate the roller coaster industry, the wooden roller coaster never completely left the scene and in the present day it exists in parallel to steel roller coasters, serving their own niche market.

Regardless of the migration to steel, the overall layout of the roller coaster hardly altered compared to its wooden predecessor. This all changed with the introduction of the first tubular coaster in 1958 by Arrow Dynamics, having a design with an entirely new track structure (Cartmell, 1987; Lanfer, 1998). Tubular coasters, as the name suggests, are shaped by a large pipe-like structure on which one can easily identify a track. The introduction of the tubular coaster led to a renewed interest in the looping, which had already been introduced earlier but failed to be a real success. The pipe-like structure made it technically easier to incorporate looping and other inversions in the overall design. In addition, the relative ease of bending steel led to the introduction of other typical thrill features of roller coasters, such as the corkscrew and suspended cars, which all deeply affected the ways in which people experience the ride.

Since the introduction of the tubular coaster there have not been other major structural changes to the underlying roller coaster design. Nevertheless, the industry has experienced many smaller and larger technological innovations ranging from the braking systems and the launching mechanism, to the way in which the carts are connected to the roller coaster track. Nowadays there is a large diversity in roller coasters offering thrills to passengers of different ages and interest. Current rides vary from the small kiddie rides and family friendly coasters, to the impressive and very fast coasters that can be found in larger theme parks around the world. The industry, and in particular the manufacturers and designers of large rides, have a strong research and development (R&D) focus to push the boundaries of technology to offer the most extreme ride possible but with safety as the primary parameter.

In the remainder of this case study, the description will be limited to companies producing steel coasters (first introduced in the early 1950s). The reason for this limitation is that while the previous wooden roller coasters did come from specialized designers, not much specialized knowledge was necessary for their construction. Since transporting wood and relocating staff is expensive and complex, the coasters were simply built by local subcontractors who were typically hired by the amusement parks. There was not a clearly identifiable roller coaster manufacturing industry before the steel coasters.

9.2.1 Identifying and Categorizing Steel Roller Coaster Manufacturers

To identify the firms that form the basis of this industry case study, this chapter relies on the online Roller Coaster Database (RCDB). This database provides a wealth of information on virtually all of the roller coasters installed worldwide and their producers/designers. An overview of the firms that form the basis of this case study is presented in Table 9.1.

Table 9.1   Roller coaster firms

Company	Country	Firm start	First roller coaster	Firm exit	Entry type	Roller coaster built	Total no. of inversions	Patents/ patent families	Unique forward citations[a]
Stengel	DE	1965	1965		D	439	524	34/5	20
Vekoma	NL	1926	1977		B	263	641	147/32	36
Zamperla	I	1966	1976		A	253	21	61/16	10
Pinfari	I	1925	1953	2007	A	162	67	12/7	9
Zierer	DE	1930	1970		A	144	1	19/7	6
Schwarzkopf	DE	1925	1955	1986	A	138	102	56/17	50
Intamin	CH	1976	1979		B	111	117	42/14	88
Mack Rides	DE	1780	1962		A	99	5	37/7	16
B&M	CH	1988	1988		D	85	351	51/9	42
Maurer Rides	DE	1865	1993		B	50	35	96/40	14
Gerstlauer	DE	1982	1992		D	46	50	12/3	13
SBF VISA	I	1952	1996		A	45	1	0/0	0
SDC	I	1965	1968	1993	A	45	0	0/0	0
L&T Systems	I	1997	1997	2009	D	35	0	2/0	0
Reverchon	FR	1929	1990	2008	A	32	0	2/1	2
Soquet	FR	1975	1980	2008	A	30	11	2/1	0

Company	Country	Firm start	First roller coaster	Firm exit	Entry type	Roller coaster built	Total no. of inversions	Patents/ patent families	Unique forward citations[a]
Giovanola/ GARW	CH	1888	1979	2003	B	24	38	11/3	16
Interpark	I	1976	1990		A	21	10	0/0	0
Fabbri	I	1950	1998		A	19	0	0	0
Iepark	I	1965	2000		A	15	1	11/3	2
Caripro	NL	1997	1997	2003	D	9	0	0/0	0
Preston	I	1986	1993		A	9	0	3/2	3
Sartori Rides	I	1950	1998	2011	A	8	3	0/0	0
Top Fun	I	1998	1998		C	8	4	0/0	0
EOS Rides	I	1995	1995		C	7	0	0/0	0
WGH ltd	UK	1989	1995		A	6	0	0/0	0
Cam Baby Car	I	1981	2002		A	4	0	0/0	0
S&MC	I	1993	1993	1997	D	4	0	5/3	0
abc-rides	CH	1997	1997		D	3	0	0/0	0
BHS	DE	1532	1986	1994	B	3	0	0/0	0
Technical Park	I	2003	2008		C	3	0	2/2	0
C&S	I	1993	1997	2000	A	1	0	0/0	0
Interlink	UK	1982	1987		A	1	0	0/0	0
Kumbak	NL	2001	2001		D	1	0	0/0	0
Ride Tek Eng.	I	2001	2001		D	1	0	6/2	3
Westech	CH	1983	2002		A	1	0	0/0	0
Professional Rides	CH	1985	2001		A	1	3	0/0	0

Notes:

[a] Excludes self-citations.

For Pinfari, SDC and Soquet we were only able to retrieve the decade in which they were established. For this analysis, we have positioned them halfway through the decade.

Some founding years and years of entry into manufacturing roller coasters are approximations, mostly estimated by information provided on the web pages of these firms.

Based on the history and product portfolio of these firms, and the pre-entry experience of the founder, it is possible to place the firms in various categories. To provide an indication of the technological expertise of firms, we complemented the above with information on: (1) the number of roller coasters the firms have built and/or designed; (2) the complexity of these rides, measured by the total number of inversions, which are the elements that turn the riders upside down and back again (looping being the most common inversion); (3) the number of roller coaster related patents the firm owns, which are obtained from patent databases; and (4) the forward citation performance of these patents (how many later patents cite patents of the firm in question). Table 9.1 shows the average scores of these different dimensions for firms in the four entry categories introduced above. Table 9.2 shows that the firms in the four different entry modes score significantly different on these dimensions. In particular, the technology diversifiers stand out by producing more coasters, producing more advanced coasters, having more patents and having a higher citation performance.

Table 9.2 Firms' characteristics by mode of entry

Entry type	Category A: Diversifier (market)	Category B: Diversifier (technology)	Category C: Parent spin-off	Category D: Entrepreneurial spin-off
Number of firms	20	5	3	9
Average number of roller coasters produced	51.70 (68.40)	90.20 (93.70)	6.00 (2.16)	69.22 (133.45)
Average number of inversions per roller coaster	0.13 (0.21)	1.15 (0.82)	0.17 (0.24)	1.05 (1.45)
Average number of patent families	10.00 (18.52)	59.20 (55.11)	0.67 (0.94)	12.56 (16.85)
Average number of cumulative forward citations	5.60 (13.02)	8.603 (33.26)	0.00 (0.00)	11.78 (18.08)

Note: Standard errors are shown in parentheses.

We now focus in more detail on these different forms of entry by investigating corresponding examples from European firms in this market. The firms we discuss are mainly from Italy, Germany, Switzerland and the Netherlands because these are the countries where most producers can be found. In this description there is a focus on the most prominent forms of entry, both in size but also in importance for the development of the industry as a whole. The section describes the firms that are classified as diversified market entrants (Category A), since these are the first entrants into the industry. Then the technological diversifiers (Category B) are presented followed by the entrepreneurial spin-offs (Category D). Parent spin-offs (Category C), as another form of entry, are not discussed in detail because of their relatively small role in the industry, both in innovation and in entrepreneurial performance.

9.2.1.1 Category A: diversified entry with market experience

As shown in Table 9.2, the majority of entrants into the steel roller coaster industry can be classified as diversifiers with market experience. This means that the product portfolio of these firms before entering the roller coaster industry included products that were sold in the same or similar markets. More specifically, most of these entrants had experience in manufacturing amusement rides such as carrousels, Ferris wheels, bumper carts and so on. By entering the roller coaster industry, these firms expanded their overall product portfolio of amusement rides. What these firms have in market experience, they often lack in technological expertise, especially compared to the technological diversifiers (see below). The lack of technological expertise is also reflected by the relatively simple design of their roller coasters. The complexity of their rides is indicated by the average number of inversion as well as their patenting intensity, which is relatively low compared to the other entrants (see Table 9.2).[1] However some firms in this category manage to acquire this expertise, either by collaborating with firms that do possess such technological competences or by acquiring resources that assist them in overcoming this problem internally. To illustrate this type of diversified entry, we now discuss two firms that can be considered exemplary for this entry type: Pinfari from Italy and Schwarzkopf from Germany.

The Italian pioneer and the first firm to ever produce a fully steel roller coaster is Pinfari. Pinfari was founded in the 1920s and produced this roller coaster in 1953. A main motive for building steel roller coasters was the need to search for alternatives to wood, which was relatively expensive. Particularly in North Italy, which lacks rich vegetation, the traditional use of wood was an even greater problem. Prior to manufacturing roller coasters, Pinfari was active in the amusement ride industry, most notably in the manufacturing and maintenance of bumper carts. Presently, the Pinfari brand is well known among roller coaster enthusiasts, mainly for manufacturing roller coasters for travelling fairs, a characteristic shared by the majority of Italian roller coaster manufacturers. Their early design appears to have inspired the first designs of other early entrants, such as SDC in Italy and Schwarzkopf in Germany; the reasons for this similarity will be explained later in this section. Pinfari was liquidated in 2004 but the brand name is still used by Interpark. In the years prior to their liquidation, a group of engineers and other key employees left the firm to start entrepreneurial spin-offs (independent from Pinfari) such as Ride Tek Engineering and DVP Rides. Overall the designs of the rides produced by Pinfari can be characterized as relatively simple, with few inversions (see Table 9.1). Furthermore, Pinfari only owned 12 patents in seven patent families, which is relatively low compared to the total number of 162 roller coasters they have produced.

The second example of diversified entry is that of Schwarzkopf in the mid-1950s. The person that headed the diversification process of Schwarzkopf, Anton Schwarzkopf, is generally regarded as one of the biggest European pioneers in roller coaster manufacturing. Prior to building roller coasters, Schwarzkopf, founded in 1924, was active in manufacturing coaches for showmen, but had already diversified to make alterations on existing amusement rides a few years before entering the roller coaster industry. An order placed by a German showman was the spark that led Schwarzkopf to produce their first (steel) roller coaster (Lanfer, 1998). Knowing that steel roller coasters were already produced in Italy, Anton Schwarzkopf made several visits to Italy to investigate this new technology ('industrial espionage'). This may partly explain why his early design closely resembled that of Pinfari's. These roller coasters were built by the Schwarzkopf's family business, owned by Anton's father. Rather unexpectedly, Schwarzkopf went bankrupt in 1983, restarted and then went bankrupt again in 1986. However, the exit of Schwarzkopf did not mean the exit of the firm's competences. Instead it led to the entry of new firms into the industry, which strengthened the position of existing firms, for example, Gerstlauer, an entrepreneurial spin-off that acquired Schwarzkopf's production facilities; Maurer Rides, which recruited former employees; and Intamin, which acquired the patents and designs.

Schwarzkopf had collaborated with the famous Werner Stengel on their first roller coaster, who worked at a Munich engineering company. Soon after this Werner Stengel would establish his own engineering company, Stengel Engineering. They continued this collaboration up to the bankruptcy of Schwarzkopf. This collaboration provided Schwarzkopf with the necessary technological competences, which explains why the rides of Schwarzkopf are more technologically advanced when compared to the above-mentioned Italian firms. Schwarzkopf produced 138 roller coasters with around 100 inversions and possessed 56 roller coaster related patents in 17 patent families.

9.2.1.2 Category B: diversified entry with technological experience

The second type of diversified entrants are those with more specialized technological experience. Their pre-entry experience is typically not related to amusement ride manufacturing, although other amusement rides might have been produced. Interestingly, these technological diversifiers, contrary to the market diversifiers, are all specialized in tubular coasters, which explains the higher number of average inversions per firm (see Table 9.2). Furthermore these firms are more active in patenting compared to other entrants, which is another indication of their technological expertise. A telling way to explain the difference between the Italian market diversifiers (and their spin-offs) and the Swiss technology diversifiers is the following: 'Italian manufacturers produce the Fiats under roller coasters and Switzerland the Mercedes' (Interview with anonymous industry expert, December 2011).

The pre-entry technological expertise we observe includes a broad set of disciplines but falls mainly within the manufacturing and design of large steel structures, piping systems, ski lifts, gondola's and transportation systems. We present a firm that is exemplary: Vekoma from the Netherlands.

Vekoma is a company with a diverse history in terms of industries. Their entrance into the roller coaster industry can be characterized as a chain of exogenous events. Repeatedly, the company experienced a decline of the industry in which they are active, forcing them to change markets (see below). During each occurrence of decline they were able to identify new markets in which they could utilize their existing technological expertise. Eventually this search for new markets led the firm into the manufacturing of roller coasters.

Founded in 1926, Vekoma started by producing equipment for the agricultural industry. With the decline of Dutch agriculture in the early 1950s, the company used its technological expertise to manufacture and construct large steel structures for the mining industry. This was a rational choice driven by the presence of the Dutch mining industry in the region. Due to the closure of the Dutch mines in the 1960s Vekoma followed their main customer, the large public company Dutch State Mines (DSM), into the petrochemical industry. As a result of the core activities of the firm they shifted their interest to the design, manufacturing and installation of piping systems. Some time later the owners recognized that this expertise could be of value in the amusement ride industry. Their first product was the Giant Wheel but soon after that they produced large tubular coasters. Vekoma grew to be one of the leading firms in the industry having produced more than 260 roller coasters, having more than 600 inversions and owning close to 150 roller coaster related patents in over 30 patent families.

Despite their position on the market, Vekoma went bankrupt in 2001. Industry experts state that this bankruptcy was the result of overinvestments in R&D in the 1990s. In combination with an increase in competition, it became more difficult to create a return on investments. Vekoma was not the only firm that experienced financial problems during this period as many large roller coaster manufacturers started to heavily invest in R&D. Other firms, including US tubular pioneer Arrow Dynamics, were forced to close down. After having restructured their debt, largely financed by Huisman Itrec, a company active in the design and manufacturing of heavy construction equipment for offshore companies, Vekoma made a restart and is now again one of the dominant players in the market.

9.2.1.3   Category D: entrepreneurial spin-off

As evidenced by Table 9.2, the second largest category is that of the entrepreneurial spin-off. As mentioned before, this type of entry involves new ventures that are not in control of an already existing firm. In contrast, they are founded by entrepreneurs that have left a firm but used the expertise obtained from the parent firm to start a new independent venture. Consequently, the entrepreneurial spin-off and the parent firm are often active within the same or similar industries and are regularly competitors. In this case study, all spin-offs can be linked to a diversifier, either market or technology based. As a result, the technological expertise is highly dependent on the technological expertise of the parent firm.

For that reason, the measures of technology complexity (inversions, patents) presented in Table 9.2 in Category D are driven by the entrepreneurial spin-offs whose parent firm had a strong technological profile, which are the technological diversifiers, like Intamin and Giovanola, and those market diversifiers that were able to acquire the necessary technological skills, like Schwarzkopf. Due to the rather recent introduction of roller coasters, in particular the tubular coasters and the complexity that is involved in manufacturing roller coasters, entrepreneurial spin-offs entered the market considerably later then diversifiers. An explanation might be that the correct competences needed to be developed by established firms before they could be of any value for new ventures. This is illustrated by providing an example of a successful Swiss entrepreneurial spin-off, Bolliger & Mabillard (B&M). Its two founders, Walter Bolliger and Claude Mabillard, established their new business in 1988, after having left Gionavala. Bolliger worked as director and Mabillard was employed as one of the main engineers. To understand their motive for starting the new venture it is important to understand the situation at their mother firm during the period of this departure. Giovanola was founded as a metal forging shop in 1888 and has a history that is rather similar to Vekoma. However Giovanola's main role was to supply roller coaster technology to other roller coaster manufacturers, primarily Intamin, who integrated their technology into their own rides. According to an industry expert, this close link with Intamin led employees to believe that they were limited in their creativity. As a result of this discontentment, Bolliger and Mabillard left the firm and B&M was founded. Interestingly, the parent firm Giovanola did not have a patent strategy so B&M was able to reproduce the roller coaster rides that were developed within Giovanola, which partly contributed to the later bankruptcy of Giovanola.

Despite its relatively late entry, B&M would become one of the leading players in the industry, producing over 85 rides. Their technological expertise is on the same level as the other large European players Vekoma, Intamin and Maurer Rides, with a total of more than 350 inversions, as well as 51 roller coaster related patents in nine patent families.

9.3   WHAT HAVE WE LEARNED?

This case of the European roller coaster industry illustrates how knowledge obtained in one particular industry can be used to exploit opportunities in other sectors.

This previous knowledge base can have different characteristics and in this particular case the knowledge base can be divided in technological competences, as illustrated in the development of the Swiss and Dutch roller coaster industry, but also market related competences, as shown to be the case in the Italian industry. The Swiss and Dutch firms only entered the industry after a large technological change in the industry, which provided the necessary opportunity for this type of firm to enter.

However, the difference in these competences has an impact on the technological complexity of the product. The Italians clearly produce products that are technologically less complex compared to the roller coasters built in Switzerland and the Netherlands. However, since amusement parks and travelling fairs demand diversity in products (since they want to offer the visitor a variety of experiences) this does not necessarily pose a problem for technologically less advanced products. They simply exist in parallel with the larger and more complex thrill rides;

after all, despite the introduction of steel and tubular coasters the wooden roller coaster is still being produced.

But how does entrepreneurship, and in particular KIE, come into the picture? There is one mode of entry where entrepreneurs play a central role. This mode is the entrepreneurial spin-off. Compared to other studies (for example, Klepper, 2009), the number of entrepreneurial spin-offs is rather limited. This might be related to the rather sophisticated knowledge that is required, but also by the very high safety standards roller coasters need to adhere to. To avoid any unnecessary risk, buyers only purchase new rides from suppliers that have a proven track record in safety, obviously hindering the establishment of new independent businesses.

The relatively small number of new businesses also indicates that not just any random former employee can and will start an entrepreneurial spin-off. Often it is the knowledgeable individuals that leave their current employer to start the entrepreneurial spin-off. In the process they take with them knowledge, work methods, reputation and sometimes their existing clients. This also explains why some of the key characteristics of the parent firm, for example, the overall organizational structure and the type of products and technologies produced, are also visible in the characteristics of their entrepreneurial spin-offs. The reasons for leaving their former employer can be manifold: sometimes it is an (imminent) bankruptcy, sometimes unhappiness with the management or the course the company is following, and sometimes they simply feel they have the ambition and quality to establish their own firm.

9.4 QUESTIONS FOR FURTHER REFLECTION

Discuss to what extent the exit of firms can lead to new venture creation.

Compare the development of the case study described in this chapter with other studies that investigate the patterns of entry into a new industry, for example, Klepper (2009), Buenstorf (2007) or the chapter on KIE in high-tech clusters by Østergaard and Park in this volume. Discuss the role of KIE in these studies and how they differ when compared to the roller coaster case.

You can access the RCDB for free (http://www.rcdb.com); this provides the opportunity to identify the overall patterns of entry of firms into the roller coaster industry. Based on this information, what can one say about the industry life cycle of the roller coaster industry? What are the phases that can be identified in this industry life cycle? What is a potential explanation for the small number of exits in the roller coaster industry?

NOTE

1. However, it is possible to see that there is some variety in the performance of these indicators from Table 9.1, and not all these firms are technologically backward.

REFERENCES

Boschma, R.A. and R. Wenting (2007), 'The spatial evolution of the British automobile industry: does location matter?', *Industrial and Corporate Change*, **16**, 213–38.

Buenstorf, G. (2007), 'Evolution on the shoulders of giants: entrepreneurship and firm survival in the German laser industry', *Review of Industrial Organization*, **30**, 179–202.

Cartmell, R. (1987), *The Incredible Scream Machine. A History of the Roller Coaster*, Wisconsin, WI: Amusement Park books and the Bowling Green State University Popular Press, University of Wisconsin Press.

Helfat, C. and M. Lieberman (2002), 'The birth of capabilities: market entry and the importance of pre-history', *Industrial and Corporate Change*, **11** (4), 725–60.

Klepper, S. (2009), 'Spinoffs: a review and synthesis', *European Management Review*, **6**, 159–71.

Klepper, S. and K. Simons (2000), 'Dominance by birthright: entry of prior radio producers and competitive ramifications in the U.S. television receiver industry', *Strategic Management Journal*, **21**, 997–1016.

Lanfer, H. (1998), *100 Jahre Achterbahn*, Reichtershausen: Gemi Verlags GmbH.

PART III

Human health care and food

PART III

Climate, Agriculture, and Food

10. How cross-fertilization of high-tech and low-tech sectors creates innovative opportunities: the case of the wearable electrocardiogram

Alexandra Rosa, Ricardo Mamede and Manuel Mira Godinho

10.1 INTRODUCTION

It is recognized that knowledge cross-fertilization, originating from different academic disciplines, companies or business sectors is a source of innovative ideas. For example, the development of Micro-Electro-Mechanical Systems (MEMS)[1] technology since the 1990s, as the interdisciplinary product of electronics, mechanical engineering, optics and chemistry, and its booming commercial applications, which range from information and communications technology (ICT) to medicine and biotechnology, is a successful illustration of knowledge interaction processes between academic and high-tech industrial teams. Also, it is acknowledged that the co-location of diverse industrial sectors in a geographical region often generates greater innovative activity outputs (Feldman and Audretsch, 1999). Further, given the increasing pace of change, competition and complexity of markets, commercial success is often found among those ventures that are able to combine knowledge in unexpected ways, thus developing cross-boundary innovative solutions for specific market needs. This includes knowledge cross-fertilization between cutting-edge technology fields and mature industries.

The case study presented in the current chapter describes the process of product development and the launching of a knowledge intensive entrepreneurship (KIE) venture operating in the cross-boundary market sector of electronic clothing. This case is focused on how the cross-fertilization of ideas and skills of people originating from unrelated knowledge fields (electronics, business management and clothing manu-facturing) and different activity sectors (academic research, high-tech business and a mature industry) contributes to the development and commercialization of a cross-boundary product. Furthermore, it shows how contrasting knowledge bases may be unconventionally integrated in order to establish an innovative business. The questions addressed by this case study are as follows:

> How can the knowledge bases of academic research, high-tech and low-tech industries be integrated to launch an innovative business?

> How can the interaction of both individuals and organizations with different areas of expertise foster cross-boundary innovations?

> Which factors may contribute to the interaction of both individuals and organizations with different areas of expertise?

10.2   THE ELECTROCARDIOGRAM T-SHIRT: FROM KNOWLEDGE CROSS-FERTILIZATION TO CROSS-BOUNDARY INNOVATION

The company under analysis was formally established in January 2007 as a spin-off from a European university research institute and is dedicated to the development and commercialization of portable electronic devices and other biomedical engineering solutions for medical diagnosis sup-port. It is a public limited company with four shareholders, as follows: an academic researcher, the spin-off's current Chief Executive Officer (CEO), a venture capital company and a university, to which the academic researcher belongs and from where the idea originated. These four shareholders are also the company's formal founders.

10.2.1   The Company: Short Overview

The core business of this spin-off firm is the development and commercialization of electronics and software engineering solutions for biomedical applications. Formally the firm is registered under the category of 'agents specialized in the sales of other particular products', NACE Code 46.180, Rev. 2.1. However, its main commercial products are electronic textile articles. More precisely, the company's key product is a smart T-shirt capable of continuously monitoring and recording a person's heart electric activity up to five days. In short, the T-shirt transforms electrocardiography equipment into a comfortable wearable device.

This apparel product is the result of a business venture originated in the collaboration between the spin-off and a large textile company. The smart T-shirt is a medical device (CE1011 marking) certified according to the European Union's (EU) Medical Devices Directive (MDD Directive 42/93/CE) and its commercial name is registered as a Community Trademark, which is owned by the university partner.

The company is targeting two market niches: health care (public and private hospitals and clinics) and sports (especially high-level sports, but also fitness). In the health care market the T-shirt has been acquired by national private practices for ambulatory monitoring of cardiac patients. On the sports segment the company is focusing on foreign European markets.

By the end of 2009 the spin-off had nine full-time employees, including the company's CEO. The recruiting process has been done gradually as new needs arise. Typically, electronics and software engineers come from the academic partner research institute as a result of institutional collaboration. But the company's staff also includes a chief finance officer (CFO), a communications and marketing director, a human resources and logistic manager and a graphics designer who is in charge of the company's web page and promotional materials design. Two of the employees hold a first degree, three a Master's degree and one a PhD.

The company's headquarters is a small building divided into two floors. The main entrance gives access to the office, which covers two distinct areas: the administration office and an open space where the marketing director, human resources manager, CFO and graphics designer have their working places. From the office, there is access to the basement, which is also divided into two areas: the electronics laboratory and the logistics sector. The latter one is where electric wires and plugs are embodied in the T-shirt and the final product is assembled.

10.2.2 From the Bedside to a Wearable Electrocardiogram Jacket

The origins of the present case study can be traced back to 2002 when the leader of a European bio-signalling laboratory decided to explore the idea of incorporating medical sensors in clothing. This researcher – henceforth called Professor – had a background in electronics and had worked with brain processing signalling during his PhD. After establishing his bio-signalling research group in 1997, he thought it would be fruitful to merge his group's expertise with the experience of the telecommunications research group of the same university. The two groups designed a joint project and the outcome of this collaboration was a telemedicine prototype developed in 2000. This prototype was a box electrocardiogram (ECG) monitor, based on PDA technology to be placed at a patient's bedside table in the hospital or at home. ECG data were collected and sent to a central point at the hospital. 'The prototype was already very near the final product', says the Professor, but it was never commercialized.

After the bedside sensor, the Professor thought that the next step would be to develop wearable ECG sensors. In the late 1990s to early 2000s technological advances in the miniaturization of electronic devices made the integration of electronics into garments more and more viable. And by that time some research and development (R&D) and business projects in this area started developing both in the USA and in Europe. The wearable ECG project of the present case study started in 2002 and evolved from a bedside box sensor to a smart jacket through electronics miniaturization, low-power microelectronics, wireless mobile technology and PDA technology. The garment design was subcontracted to the national technology centre for the textile and clothing industries,[2] under the specifications defined by the Professor's research team. The first prototype, designed as a jacket, was released in 2006. This prototype was the basis of a new venture, which in many regards may be considered a typical university spin-off.

10.2.3 The Prototype Evolves

Nonetheless, the resemblance between this prototype and the company's smart T-shirt, launched in 2009, is almost solely in the device's concept. In the jacket version, the clothing was made of two pieces: a thick T-shirt and an unwashable jacket that carried all the electronics, which were by then much bigger and heavier than the current electronics unit. Both items (T-shirt and jacket) were connected by a plug. Also, the smart jacket was an ECG monitor and much more. It measured almost every physiological activity: respiratory rate, body temperature, haemoglobin oxygen saturation, physical activity through an incorporated monitor (actigraph), and had a panic button. Later, during the development phase of the spin-off, the company partners decided to focus on just one type of sensor. And electrocardiography was acknowledged as the most important. Still, the jacket prototype was a success. The smart garment was shown in national and international technical textile fairs and the country's media widely reported on the electronics jacket.

By the end of 2006, after the smart jacket prototype was released, a series of conditions enabled the establishment of a spin-off company. First, the product concept had attained enough technological maturity.

Second, a food consulting entrepreneur – henceforth called CEO – who was a close friend of the Professor was available and had the motivation to be the head of a new business venture. This condition was essential for establishing the spin-off because the Professor did not want to leave academia or his research group for a full-time activity in a business enterprise. He says: 'Asking me to become a company's CEO is the worst thing anyone could ask me for.' Today, he still leads his university research group, but he keeps working as a R&D consultant to the spin-off, where he holds a non-executive position. Finally, a venture capital company co-founded by one of the Professor's former research colleagues was willing to invest 0.5 million euros in this business project.

As the necessary conditions – product technology, managerial capability provided by an available and reliable CEO and financial resources – were set, the spin-off was established in the beginning of 2007. But the company's product – the smart garment – had to be reinvented.

When the T-shirt concept was developed it was targeted to the health care market. However, this market was difficult to enter and the entrepreneurs decided to move to the sports market, which involved redesigning all the technology and the clothing. The initial prototype had been developed for static measurements, like a patient's clinical test. But as users in sports are moving all the time, both the electronics and garment had to be redesigned to a more flexible device. In technological terms, it meant a change from a two-dimensional frame to a three-dimensional one and this implied that almost everything had to be reinvented. However, after the readjustment of the initial concept the health care market became receptive to the company's product. The CEO says: 'The problem is that the prototype was unsuitable for commercialization. We used the concept, but had to remake everything.'

10.2.4 In Search for the Right Textile Partner

During the company's first year, the CEO – by that time the company was just him and his computer – focused only on market research. He knew that he had to find a textile partner soon. 'We mastered the electronics, but we needed a textile partner that could develop with us the garment in an industrial perspective,' says the CEO. The location of the spin-off facilitated, to a large extent, the search process – this is a region with a long tradition in the production of textiles and clothing. Still, it took several months of disappointing meetings with different textile companies until the CEO finally met the head of a firm who, according to him, had 'an incredible capacity of looking forward and had already

Table 10.1 Entrepreneurs: who's who

The Professor (b. 1967)	Holds a PhD in electrotechnical engineering. Since his undergraduate studies, in electronics and telecommunications, he 'got passionate by' biomedical research. Indeed, his PhD thesis was in brain signal processing and he focused on epilepsy studies. In 1997, he founded a research group on health care information systems, which he still leads. Although the outputs of his research projects have had a commercialization potential, the Professor has never had the motivation to leave the laboratory bench as he doesn't picture himself as a businessman. 'I wouldn't survive in the business environment. I'd go mad with all those management meetings,' he says. The Professor holds a non-executive position at the spin-off and he is the company's R&D consultant.
The CEO (b. 1976)	Holds a PhD in food biotechnology. During his research work, he became aware that many university researchers didn't acknowledge the market potential of their research output. He says: 'There are plenty of research projects which show very promising technology. But those ideas are normally disclosed as research papers.' This motivated him to go into industry and in 2003 he established a food consulting company, his first business venture. In 2007, when the present case spin-off was founded, the Professor called for his entrepreneurship know-how and motivation. 'We had known each other for a long time and after the food consulting company it was time that I moved on to another business venture,' says the CEO, who defines himself as a very practical person.
The Investor (b. 1969)	Holds a Master's in electrotechnical engineering. He was an electronics researcher for two years at the Professor's research institute. But unlike the Professor, he feels fulfilled in the business environment and comfortable with the practical aspects of entrepreneurship. He has been a business associate and co-founder of several information technology (IT) companies. In 2006, he co-founded the venture capital company that is the financial partner of the spin-off.

realized the promising potential of electronic clothing'. In a fortnight the spin-off and the textile company had signed a contract agreement for both companies to work together in the production of the new garment.

The textile partner is a European textile enterprise, which has developed an innovative technological process of making seamless clothing. In this process, the fabrics are glued together instead of being sewn. This technology is mostly used in sports, namely in swimming suits. This company has been established for more than 20 years, has about a thousand employees and manufactures 20 000 textile pieces per day on an original equipment manufacturer (OEM) basis.

The ECG T-shirt development process was interactive and it progressed on two fronts: electronics and textiles. The electronics development consisted mainly in the upgrading of the ECG sensors technology and software, which was done with the collaboration of the Professor's academic research group and the spin-off's four software engineers, recruited in 2008. On the textile front, the design of the garment was assigned to the textile company, but the process was closely followed by the CEO. The main idea was to simplify the initial garment (a jacket connected to a T-shirt). The CEO recalls the process: 'We started by simplifying the prototype until the jacket became a T-shirt. And then we started simplifying the T-shirt. First, is was a T-shirt with a belt for carrying the electronics, then the electronics were in a box and there was a pocket to put the box in, then the belt had a pocket for the box ... and in the end it was only a T-shirt.'

10.2.5   The ECG T-shirt

The innovation of this case study consists of a new to the market ECG T-shirt wireless monitor, which is able to trace a person's heart rate for up to five days. The electronics of this wearable ECG were engineered to a lightweight (50 g) miniaturized (66 x 38 x 16 mm) measuring unit, which is placed in a dedicated pocket inside the T-shirt. The heart events are registered in the unit's memory card. This enables ECG visualization in a desktop or laptop computer, but also in a personal digital assistant (PDA). Additionally, as the measuring unit is provided with Bluetooth connectivity, it is possible to visualize live and remotely the ECG tracing via General Packet Radio Service (GPRS). Also, the unit displays a simple and visible colour code that allows easy interpretation by both health practitioners and patients. In fact, all the software associated with the device is user friendly not only to health practitioners but also a wider audience, including elderly people, who are target users in the health market.

A set of three electric wires is embedded in the T-shirt, allowing the user to measure the ECG in a comfortable way. That is, without feeling the wires dangling while carrying out one's daily activities. This is one the major advantages of this smart T-shirt. In contrast to other mobile ECG monitors (namely, the commercial Holter monitor), the discomfort caused by wires dangling was removed. The users – especially elderly people and athletes – are able to maintain their normal activities, including practising sports and sleeping, which makes this ECG a minimum intrusive device.

From the clinical point of view, the non-intrusive aspect is an important gain as it allows for the measurement of the true activity of the heart in cardiac patients. This is mainly because the patients can perform their daily routines in a comfortable way, while having their heart monitored. To measure heart activity, three electrodes are placed in three zones of the user's body. After putting on the T-shirt, the electrodes are fixed to three springs connected to each of the electric wires. A plug in the other end of the wires connects the system to the measuring unit.

The T-shirt itself is totally glued together, without seams, using the patented technology of the textile company. This further enhances the T-shirt's comfort, which is an important bonus of this medical device. The garment – 80 per cent polyamide, 20 per cent elastane – is completely washable and available in female (three sizes) and male (four sizes) versions. The T-shirt was designed in black for clinical proposes (to be used as underwear) and in more colourful patterns for sports and fitness. The product is sold in a cardboard box with the following items: T-shirt, a measuring unit (including the memory card), 25 disposable electrodes, a battery recharger and a CD with the software analysis pack.

Despite what has been achieved, the company – in collaboration with its university partner and the textile company – is continuously improving the T-shirt's technology and launching new products, like a ECG baby suit, and the development of other biomedical sensors, for example, stress and tracking monitors dedicated to firemen. According to the CEO 'The best strategy is time leadership.'

10.2.6 Medical Testing and Certification

During the development process, the ECG T-shirt was being continuously tested in public and private hospitals, a regular practice that was inherited from the Professor's earlier research experience. According to him, 'In our projects there is always a lot of involvement of the clinical staff. I don't believe in doing things only at the university. Even during my PhD, I spent more time in hospitals than at the university.' Concomitantly, the T-shirt's medical certification process started in the middle of 2008, a lengthy step-by-step procedure, which took more than one year to be concluded. Finally, by the end of 2009 the ECG T-shirt was awarded a Medical Device Conformité Européenne (CE)[3] marking and it was ready to be commercialized. For the CEO, it was time 'to start selling the T-shirts'.

10.3 WHAT HAVE WE LEARNED FROM THE CASE OF THE WEARABLE ECG?

Throughout this case study it has been described how cross-fertilization across diverse economic sectors (academia–industry, high tech–low tech) and different knowledge bases (electronics, telecommunications, medicine, computer science, textile technology, clothing design, management, marketing) can be integrated into novel ways to find innovative product solutions for new market needs. In fact, since the bench research phase to the commercialization of the ECG T-shirt, relevant interactions between different sectors and different knowledge bases were observed in this case study. Table 10.2 summarizes the different types of sectors and knowledge bases identified throughout the development to the launch of the company and the commercialization of the smart T-shirt.

Table 10.2   Sectors and knowledge bases involved in the ECG T-shirt KIE venture

KIE phase		Knowledge base	Sector involved
Background	Lab research	Bio-signalling and telecommunications	University research centre
	Bedside monitor	Telemedicine	University research centre
Development 1	ECG jacket	Telemedicine, electronics and textiles	University research centre and textiles technology centre
Company launching		Management and market prospect	Electronic engineering, university research centre and financial company
Development 2	ECG T-shirt	Electronics, software, ITC, textile technology, clothing design and marketing	Electronic engineering, textiles company and university research centre
Product testing and certification	ECG T-shirt	Bio-electronics, clothing design and health care	Electronics engineering, textiles company and health care centres
Product commercialization	ECG T-shirt	Marketing communication	Electronic clothing

By reading Table 10.2, and as described in the case study, one perceives that the wearable ECG is the result of the successful interaction of rather distinct economic sectors and knowledge bases. According to Fleming

(2004), a way to reduce the chances of failure of innovations resulting from the cross-pollination of unrelated knowledge areas is 'to bring together people with deep, rather than broad, expertise in their respective disciplines'. This case is a good illustration of this hypothesis. As described, the major actors involved in the present KIE process had a deep expertise in their respective fields, particularly the actors involved in the two more distant areas, namely telemedicine and textiles. The Professor and his research group brought the expertise in bio-measurements, electronics and telecommunications, while the textile company brought the know-how on industrial production, textile technology and design. But also on the management side, the CEO contributed with his successful past experience as an entrepreneur and the venture capital company with financial resources and management expertise. Finally, at an earlier stage the textile technology centre was also instrumental in helping to develop the product concept.

This case study also illustrates all the evolution stages of a product from its early concept to its commercialization in order to create a real business opportunity. This process involved matching an inventive concept with scientific and technological knowledge, production knowledge and market opportunities: the wearable ECG was first conceptualized as a multifunctional bio-monitor wearable device targeted at the health care market, which was later designed as an ECG T-shirt targeted at the sports market and finally commercialized in both the health care and sports markets.

Moreover, this case study highlights how more mature technological sectors, normally classified as low-tech sectors, can be involved in cutting-edge innovations.

Finally, the case study shows how the geographical proximity between scientific and technical organizations (namely universities, technological centres and hospitals) with apparently unrelated industrial activities (in the present case, textiles and clothing) can foster innovation through the cross-fertilization of their knowledge bases.

10.4 QUESTIONS FOR FURTHER REFLECTION

In your opinion, could the type of knowledge interaction described in this case study be generalized to other industries? Which ones? Give examples.

Henderson and Clark (1990) proposed an intermediate categorization of innovation, between incremental and radical innovation, called architectural innovation. They defined architectural innovations as 'innovations that change the architecture of a product without changing its components.' Discuss the innovation of this case under Henderson and Clark's definition of 'architectural innovation'.

This case ends in 2009, just after the initial commercialization of the ECG T-shirt. Design a follow-up study of this case, focusing on the factors that could be limiting or contributing to the commercial success of this innovation.

NOTES

1. MEMS are microscopic mechanical devices, fabricated on silicon chips similarly to integrated circuits. MEMS can be used as miniaturized sensors, actuators or other micro devices. Microsensors and microactuators are called 'transducers', which are devices that convert energy from one form to another. In the case of microsensors, the device typically converts a measured mechanical signal into an electrical signal. MEMS applications include medical disposable pressure sensors and biochips for DNA identification. See http://www.memsnet.org/news/ (accessed 17 June 2012).
2. This technology centre is a private, non-profit institution that operates mainly under public support.
3. CE marking states that the product is assessed before being placed on the market and meets EU safety, health and environmental protection requirements (http://ec.europa.eu/enterprise/policies/single-market-goods/cemarking/).

REFERENCES

Feldman, M.P. and D.B. Audretsch (1999), 'Innovation in cities: science-based diversity, specialization and localized competition', *European Economic Review*, **43**, 409–29.

Fleming, L. (2004), 'Perfecting cross-pollination', *Harvard Business Review*, **82** (9), 22–4.

Henderson, R.M. and K.B. Clark (1990), 'Architectural innovation: the reconfiguration of existing product technologies and the failure of established firms', *Administrative Science Quarterly*, **35**, 9–22.

11. Building collaborative network relationships: the case of a corporate spin-off in the medical technology industry

Jens Laage-Hellman

11.1 INTRODUCTION

This case study is about Otocare Ltd, a European corporate spin-off company in the medical technology ('medtech') industry, and focuses on the building of network relationships with different types of external actors. It is well known that in business-to-business markets trading to a large extent takes place within more or less close and long-term business relationships (between sellers and buyers). In addition, such relationships are frequently used for the purpose of technological innovation. In that context, besides interacting with business partners, collaboration with academia may be necessary in order to gain access to new knowledge and competence.

For natural reasons, the KIE start-up companies created, for example, to commercialize new inventions, to a large extent lack this type of relationships when they are founded. Therefore, during the early phase of their development major efforts typically have to be made in order to build relationships.

The present case study thus addresses the issue of relationship-building from the perspective of a corporate spin-off. For example, why is the building of collaborative relationships with external actors important to corporate start-ups? Which are the most important types of partners and why? What type of problems and difficulties may the companies encounter in their networking?

11.2   CASE DESCRIPTION

Otocare, now sold to another firm, manufactured and marketed a unique, bone-anchored hearing aid invented jointly by technical and medical researchers. It uses a metallic implant in combination with a hearing device attached to the implant on the outside of the head.

11.2.1   Pre-history

The idea behind the bone-anchored hearing aid had arisen at a university hospital, where an ear surgeon at the ear, nose and throat (ENT) clinic was instrumental in developing the whole method including, for example, the surgical procedure. This work started in the late 1970s and continued for many years. Initially, the commercialization took place in an existing firm, Dentia, which was a pioneer in osseo-integrated dental implants. From 1985 Dentia worked on the bone-anchored hearing aid, which uses the same type of implant, in close collaboration with the inventing academics. The technical researchers owned through their own company some key patents for the device and also became heavily involved as consultants.

Initially, the research carried out at the ENT clinic was extremely important for the development of the method. However, the importance of this clinic decreased over time. Instead, there were two other hospitals located abroad that emerged as leading centers for research on the bone-anchored hearing aid. A large number of clinical tests were carried out at these two centers and they became important partners for the company.

In 1988, the bone-anchored hearing aid got approval for reimbursement in the domestic market, and this proved that the method had begun to be clinically accepted. The market potential for Europe and the USA was estimated to be around 40 million euros. However, despite intensified marketing efforts and reimbursement obtained in an increasing number of countries, sales increased only slowly. It took time, for example, to convince physicians about the benefits of the product, to train them and to start up clinical studies.

The ENT clinic was helpful in spreading knowledge about the method and educating physicians. The inventing ear surgeon in particular played a key role as a door opener and helped the company establish contacts with other clinics around the world. There was increasing interest in the method and it was not too difficult to find clinics that were willing to start up clinical studies. The problem was how to finance the studies. Sometimes the costs had to be covered by the company. However, the budget was limited and this affected the number of studies. Another problem was that the company did not have internal competence in medical affairs related to hearing aids.

By the mid-1990s, sales of the bone-anchored hearing aid had reached around 400 000 euros. In 1996, however, an important breakthrough was made when Dentia after seven to eight years of hard work obtained product approval in the USA.

11.2.2 Foundation of Otocare

For Dentia the dental implants constituted the core business. The hearing aids business had a smaller market potential. In addition, both the product and the market were of a different kind and were perceived to be complex.

Over the years, Dentia made several attempts to sell the hearing aids project, but these plans came to nothing. However, in 1997 after Dentia had gone public, the top management decided that Dentia should become a fully dedicated 'dentistry company.' As preparation for the sale of the hearing aids business a business plan for a conceivable new company was made. It assumed a rapid increase in turnover reaching 14 million euros in three years.

The presentation of the business to potential investors was well received and in January 1999 two venture capital (VC) firms decided to buy in. Each of them took a 20 percent share of the new company, while Dentia kept 60 percent. The latter had started to realize that the hearing aids business could have a promising future. However, unlike the other two investors, Dentia became a passive owner. The investment in Otocare was seen as purely financial and during the following years the ownership share was gradually reduced.

At the time of foundation Otocare had 25 employees. An accumulated number of around 7000 patients had received the implant and in 1998 the business area had reached sales amounting to 3.3 million euros. During the spring of 1999, the personnel were moved out of Dentia's premises and a sales-oriented and experienced manager with an international background was recruited as Chief Executive Officer (CEO). In connection to his arrival he sent the following message to the personnel:

> Otocare is now a truly independent company. Our attention is totally focused on our customers and their needs. Our future success depends on the continuous development of our relationships with all those who use our product systems. We will only be as good as you perceive us to be!

During the first year (1999) Otocare reached 4.7 million euros in sales.

11.2.3 Developments in Otocare from 2000 to 2005

The establishment of Otocare meant that more resources became available for research and development (R&D). Increasing efforts were made both in product development and clinical research. The latter was especially important as a means to develop new indications and enlarge the potential market.

Thus, the intensified development activities resulted in a number of new product launchings that helped boost sales. For example, there were new implant solutions and surgical tools that made the operation easier for the surgeons. There were other products that made it possible to reach new market segments.

Approval of reimbursement in different countries was an important driver of sales. This is usually a slow process where the company is dependent on national authorities and insurance companies. Here, Otocare could draw on previous work carried out by Dentia.

The intensified sales activities, including increasing research collaboration with key customers around the world, resulted in accelerated sales development, and more people were employed. The number of patients operated on increased steadily. The number of sold devices increased even more. This was partly due to the introduction of an insurance replacement program.

Table 11.1 summarizes the development of turnover and staff over time.

Table 11.1   Development of sales and staff over time

	1998 (before spin off from Dentia)	1999 (first year after spin off)	2002	2004 (before trade sale)	2010 (new owner)
No. of employees		25	100		200
Turnover (million euros)	3.3	4.7	13.5	24	48.5

11.3 RELATIONSHIP-BUILDING ACTIVITIES

The following deals more specifically with the relationship-building activities in three different settings: use, production and science. For each the course of events are described more or less in chronological order. It should be noted that these are parallel processes, which means that there will be some inevitable jumping in time.

11.3.1 Relationships with Users/Customers

During the Dentia period the hearing aids team was engaged in various clinical activities so that at the time of foundation, Otocare had established collaborative relationships with a range of clinics around the world, some of which were sponsored by the company. In addition, the new company extended its resources for R&D. These were used for clinical studies as well as product development.

11.3.2 Widening the Application Field

A particularly important goal for the clinical research pursued by Otocare was to widen the use of the method by developing new indications. The bone-anchored hearing aid had originally been developed for treatment of patients with certain types of two-sided conductive hearing loss, and this was the indication on which the original market potential had been calculated. However, it was realized that there existed a much larger market potential if the method could be used for other indications. In particular, there was potential to use the product to treat single-sided deafness – an often overlooked problem for which no effective treatment existed.

The potential market for this indication was four times larger than for the conductive hearing loss. The US market was particularly big due to clinical practices that differed from what was common in Europe.

The idea of using the bone-anchored hearing aid for single-sided deafness was not new, and it had been practiced to some limited extent. A first clinical study had been carried out by one hospital and this had helped generate interest. But there was a need for more studies. Initially the ear surgeon, using his vast contact network, was helpful in putting Otocare in contact with American clinics. These included two hospitals that carried out important clinical studies showing the benefits of the method.

Given the great importance of capturing this market, Otocare took the initiative to finance a large, international multicenter study. A standardized protocol was written by Otocare and used by all participants. It was the company that merged the data and submitted an application to the Food and Drug Administration. The application was cleared in September 2002 and meant that Otocare could start selling its product. As a result, sales accelerated, not just in the USA, and single-sided deafness became the dominant application.

Otocare's CEO took a very active part in these activities, which were of strategic importance to future growth. The clinical contacts arranged by the ear surgeon were taken over by the company and were further developed into fruitful clinical collaborations. Hard work was required to become familiar with the clinical partners and build credibility for the company. The potential partners already had good contacts with their colleagues at the ENT clinic, but in order to get the collaboration going a trustful relationship had to be established with the company itself. By its own means, Otocare established collaborations with other hospitals.

Interestingly, the pioneering ENT clinic did not play an important role in this development. The Audiology Unit of the hospital, which controlled the clinical use of the method, was not convinced about its benefits for this indication and therefore the regional health care authority did not reimburse the treatment. This limited the possibility of carrying out clinical research.

11.3.3 The Relationship between Otocare and the Pioneering ENT Clinic

From the ear surgeon's perspective, the relationship with the company did not change much when the business was spun off from Dentia and became Otocare. He continued to support the company, for example, by receiving customers, delivering lectures at company-sponsored workshops and visiting other clinics in connection with the start up of clinical studies. He was also valuable in giving clinical advice and reviewing surgical manuals.

In order to compensate the ear surgeon for his extra work and expenses, the company had a consultancy agreement with him. These activities were openly presented as a financial disclosure at scientific conferences.

The company had occasionally given small research grants to the university hospital, but in general had not paid for clinical studies. Such work was seen as a normal part of the health care task.

The ear surgeon notes that it became easier for the company to run clinical studies after the formation of Otocare and the implementation of a new, more ambitious development strategy. That was a positive change from his point of view. During the Dentia era it had been difficult to raise money for non-dental activities and in reality decisions had been taken by the corporate management (rather than by the business area management). In Otocare it was different. First, there was more money available for R&D. Second, the CEO had full freedom to take decisions. With his background in marketing and sales, he had a good understanding of the need to involve customers and personally engaged himself in these activities.

The ear surgeon retired a few years ago but is still active, for example, by giving lectures. However, the responsibility for the therapeutic and research activities related to the bone-anchored hearing aid has been taken over by two younger physicians.

As described, the ENT clinic played a crucial role in the invention of bone-anchored hearing aids and the development of the method. However, for many years there have been other hospitals, mainly abroad, that have become more important as clinical partners. This is to a large extent due to the number of patients treated with the method. Due to different reimbursement policies there are thus other hospitals that offer better opportunities for clinical collaboration.

11.3.4 Relationships with Suppliers

11.3.4.1 Implant

The implant was initially produced in Dentia's own plant. However, this plant was not used to handle external customers and Otocare therefore wanted to take over the production. At the same time, Dentia was not interested in continuing to produce the hearing aid implant, since the volume was low and the costs were high. For Otocare it was crucial to secure supply of the implant until a new production solution was in place. To allow enough time for the transfer a three-year supply agreement was signed.

One of Otocare's alternatives was to build up an in-house facility. However, it chose instead to move production to another supplier. It had to be a company dedicated to serve external customers. Given the relatively small volume and the complexity of the product, which necessitated close interaction initially, there was a need to find a supplier that was not only competent but also willing to invest the resources needed to solve all technical problems. Otocare knew that a small customer is not prioritized. There were several alternatives, and this included one foreign company. But the final choice became the domestic MediTech, which had a plant close by. MediTech had specialized in subcontracting implants and other medical devices and was therefore a suitable supplier. MediTech also turned out to be willing to supply.

Transferring production to the new supplier was not unproblematic, however. MediTech had bigger technical problems than expected and Otocare therefore had to devote a great deal of time and efforts to support the supplier. In fact, it took the two companies more than one year of joint preparation and testing to solve all the problems. Here, the geographical proximity between the two firms was a great advantage since it facilitated frequent contacts.

11.3.4.2 Hearing device

When Otocare was founded in 1999 the in-house assembly of the hearing device was transferred to Otocare, which also took over existing suppliers. This included the most central component, a vibrating transducer, the manufacturing of which had been outsourced to the technical researchers through their own company. However, the management of Otocare, to prepare the company for the owners' future exit, wanted to take over the manufacturing of the vibrator – thereby eliminating the company's dependence (for a critical component) on the technical researchers. By making the company 'clean' from such dependencies it would be easier to sell it, it was thought. The negotiations with the researchers were tough. The researchers were strongly committed to the product, on which they had spent a great deal of time and also made money. At the end, after 18 months of negotiations, a new agreement was finally reached according to which the manufacturing responsibility was transferred to Otocare. In return, Otocare would pay royalties to the researchers. This deal made them happy since they would no longer have to spend time on the vibrator but still earn some money.

Otocare initially decided to transfer the manufacturing of the vibrator to a new subcontractor. The manufacturing was still rather manual. The new supplier, however, encountered a lot of technical problems. It was realized that the vibrator is a sensitive component that is difficult to produce. Otocare therefore decided to in-source production and build up a highly automated production line. Besides solving the quality problems, this also enabled the company to increase the volume and exploit scale advantages. This was needed in order to meet the increasing demand.

11.3.5　Relationships with Academic Researchers

Otocare has interacted with two types of academic environments. One is the university clinics. They are at the same time part of the use setting and the company's collaboration with them has been described above. Otocare also had an important relationship with a small group of technical researchers. They had made crucial contributions to the development of the product by inventing various parts of the hearing device. In the early days these researchers performed the company's function of technical development and were also responsible for production and clinical trials. They did this as consultants working through their own firm, which also owned key patents exclusively licensed to Dentia, and later to Otocare.

It was not until 1993 that Dentia began to take over full responsibility for the device. But the license agreement remained effective and the researchers, through their own company, continued to supply the vibrator.

Thus, when Otocare was formed in 1999 the technical researchers were no longer engaged as consultants, but the new company inherited the license agreement for the device as a whole and the subcontracting agreement for the vibrator. How this supply arrangement was winded up has been described above.

The technical researchers have continued their research focusing on the next generation of (implantable) hearing aid. The company performed joint activities with the researchers in this context, but after a couple of years chose to terminate the collaboration. It preferred to concentrate its own resources on the current product. Since then the contacts with the researchers have been limited.

11.3.6　Trade Sale of Otocare in 2005

In 2002, Otocare had basically reached its goal as formulated in the three-year business plan prepared before the spin-off. Sales had increased to 13.5 million euros and the company had around 100 employees. The accumulated number of patients had risen to 12 000 and the trend indicated continued growth.

The two VC firms had plans to make an exit. They made some attempts to sell the company in the fall of 2002, but they found that this was not the best timing. The profitability of Otocare was not high enough. To prepare the company for a more profitable exit the management therefore decided to cut certain costs, for example, related to long-term development projects, and to prioritize sales and profits.

Two years later, in the spring of 2005, an agreement was reached to sell Otocare for 135 million euros to another manufacturer of hearing aids. Otocare had reached 24 million euros in sales by 2004. The buying firm had successfully commercialized another type of implant that targeted another type of hearing loss.

The bone-anchored hearing aids business is now run from the same headquarters as before but under a new name. The growth rate continues to be high.

11.3.7 New License Agreement

The license agreement with the technical researchers had been signed in 1985 and remained unchanged over the years. However, after Otocare had been sold in 2005 the new management took the initiative to renegotiate. At this time there was a patent portfolio consisting of 18 patents, some of which were owned by the researchers and others by the company. The parties had agreed to cross-usage of these patents. The renegotiation that took place resulted in a new license agreement according to which the company could use all patents related to the bone-anchored hearing aid for free. In return, the technical researchers got the rights to all patents related to the next generation device.

11.4 WHAT HAVE WE LEARNED?

The first subsection below addresses the questions raised in the introduction:

> Why is the building of collaborative relationships with external actors important to start-ups?
>
> Which are the most important types of partners and why?
>
> What type of problems and difficulties may the companies encounter in their networking?

The second subsection gives a short comment on the advantages of spinning out the business by the formation of Otocare.

11.4.1 The Importance of Relationship-building for Start-ups

This case study, including some developments taking place in Dentia before the foundation of Otocare, confirms the importance of relationship-building in the context of knowledge intensive entrepreneurship. Most importantly, the establishment of collaborative relationships with business partners in the use and production settings is a crucial element of the innovation process. Thus, teaming up with customers or end-users is often necessary both in order to develop the product itself and introduce it into the market. This holds true especially for products that are radically new. Then, there is often a great need for the innovating firm to explore how the product should be designed in order to fit into its context of use and how it should be used (that is, development of application knowledge). There may also be a need, by testing the product under real-life conditions, to produce evidence about the benefits of the new product (compared to existing solutions).

When Otocare was founded a set of collaborative relationships with various clinical partners were already in place. Nonetheless, the commercial (and economic) success of Otocare necessitated further efforts to develop existing relationships and establish new ones. This became, for example, an essential task for the CEO himself who spent much of his time interacting with clinical partners. This also points to the importance of staffing start-ups, at an early stage, with marketing-oriented managers (rather than R&D people).

The importance of using indirect relationships is nicely illustrated. Otocare historically had a close relationship with a clinical scientist, who was one of the inventors of the method. This person was instrumental by using his own contact network to help Otocare establish collaborations with other prominent clinics around the world – something that was necessary in order to further develop the method and get it accepted in the market. But once the contact with a potential partner had been established the company took over the responsibility for managing the relationship. This is, however, a resource-demanding task. In order to build trustful and effective collaborative relationships with clinical partners the start-up needs to acquire internal competence in medical affairs.

Turning to the production setting, the case study also shows that in order to manufacture the new product external suppliers of key components may need to be involved in the technical development. Like many other medtech start-ups Otocare chose to outsource much of the production. This included the device and later also the implant. Various design-related production problems had to be solved jointly by the customer and the supplier and this necessitated close relationships.

Generally, new start-ups may have difficulties attracting interest of potential suppliers when there is a need to make customer-specific adaptations of the component to be purchased. This is because initially the volume is very low and the whole business often has an uncertain future. In addition, the buying firm tends to have scarce resources and lacks internal competence. The supplier's reluctance to make their own investments on behalf of such a customer is understandable. Corporate spin-offs may have an advantage compared to other types of start-ups. Thus, some supplier relationships may already have been established by the parent company, which may be seen as a more reliable and attractive customer. If new supplier relationships need to be established after the spin-off, the company has an ongoing business and a track record to refer to.

Regarding the science setting, there was also a need to develop the relationship with the academic partners – both in the medical and technical fields. Note that the clinical collaborators are not only scientists but also representatives of the user side.

In this case study, Otocare had inherited a unique relationship with the inventing technical researchers, who for a long time had been intensively involved in the business, both as a provider of knowledge and as a supplier of a critical component (via their own company). For Otocare, this strong dependence on the researchers was not acceptable, for example, given the company's long-term growth plans. However, when taking over control of this component it turned out to be difficult to transfer the production to another supplier, and in the end Otocare had to in-source. This illustrates that finding an external production solution may not always be easy if the invention to be commercialized incorporates unique elements.

11.4.2   The Advantages of a Spin-off

The idea behind the bone-anchored hearing aid was initially developed in an existing firm. Despite a periodically ambivalent attitude from the corporate management, it seems that after all this was a good solution – compared to having the invention commercialized by starting up a totally new firm. Nonetheless, it must be concluded that spinning out Otocare from Dentia at a later time was probably beneficial to long-term development and growth. The hearing aids business was of a different kind to Dentia's core business. Therefore, it did not receive full attention from the corporate management and had to compete internally for resources. By creating a dedicated firm funded by owners who saw the potential and were committed to building a high-growth company, it became in many ways easier for the management to develop the business and exploit existing market opportunities. The success of Otocare indicates that making a corporate spin-off was the right thing to do. With hindsight it also seems that the timing was good.

11.5 QUESTIONS FOR FURTHER REFLECTION

The Otocare case study deals with the networking of a research-based corporate spin-off. It exemplifies some of the general challenges that new entrepreneurial ventures have to cope with, especially in the early phase of their life. There is no doubt that establishing and developing network relationships is a strategically important activity for such firms – in order to achieve commercial success. However, what we need to know more about is how this should be done. Put differently, is it possible to identify success factors that help company managers to network more effectively? The Otocare case gives some hints, but there is definitely a need for more research on this topic.

Another question that merits further discussion and inquiry has to do with the role of public policy. In other words, what can policy actors do in order to support this type of networking and achieve positive growth effects?

The existence of differences regarding networking prerequisites and challenges among different types of start-ups is another issue that could be further elaborated. Besides corporate spin-offs there are university spin-offs, coming from different types of research environments, and start-ups founded by independent entrepreneurs. To what extent do they differ in terms of networking?

12. Collaborative research in innovative food: an example of renewing a traditional low-tech industry

Maureen McKelvey, Daniel Ljungberg and Jens Laage-Hellman

12.1 INTRODUCTION

This chapter presents a case study of how collaborative research can help renew a traditional low-tech industry, namely the agriculture and food industry. Low-tech industries imply that the industry spends a small percentage of sales on research and development (R&D) activities. Many low-tech industries, such as the food industry, are dominated by larger firms, often organizing a global value chain, but they also interact with smaller firms and cooperatives offering specific components in that value chain or specialized products and services. In low-tech industries, the renewal of the industries may come from start-up companies offering particular services, but large firms play a major role. Renewal also takes place through corporate entrepreneurship inside large firms and collaborative research between large firms, small firms and universities. This chapter therefore focuses on how collaborative research helps develop scientific and technological knowledge for innovative foods, and discusses how primarily the larger firms then develop those ideas into market and business knowledge through new products and services.

Innovative food represents a way to develop higher value-added products and services, with trends in recent decades including areas like 'functional foods', 'intelligent foods', 'ecological/green products' and 'nutritionals'. In this chapter, we use the concept of 'innovative food' to represent attempts by the industry, in collaboration with universities and public policy organizations, to stimulate more competitive products and goods. We focus on the effects of particular public policy initiatives to stimulate collaborative research in this area. They were designed to stimulate the development of a series of related products, competencies, specific technologies, instruments and measuring techniques. The new scientific and technological knowledge is often linked to broad societal goals and results from developments in specific technological fields, such as sensors and biomarkers. To prove health care benefits such knowledge may, for example, be necessary in order to identify the characteristics of the grain being used in food production.

The role of public policy is interesting in this case, as the investigated initiative that stimulated corporate entrepreneurship and knowledge intensive entrepreneurship (KIE) within the industry was explicitly based on enhancing interaction and collaboration between academic research institutes and firms. Public industrial policy has during the last few decades increasingly focused on the objective to stimulate innovation as a means of economic and societal progress (Lundvall and Borrás, 2005). Today it is generally recognized that the innovation process is systematic and interactive, with the need for networks and collaboration among different types of actors. Universities and academic research institutes have increasingly been considered important actors in this systematic and interactive innovation process, and have therefore been the subject of much policy efforts (Mowery and Sampat, 2005). It is thought that the increasing flow of new scientific knowledge and competencies will benefit a country's own industry and improve the prerequisites for long-term development and growth. In this way, public policy to a large extent focuses on 'inducing' and stimulating interaction and collaboration between industry and universities. This chapter addresses the following questions:

> In what ways can new scientific and technological knowledge help stimulate renewal of products and services in traditional low-tech industries like food?

> What are the expected benefits to firms from participating in collaborative research?

12.2 COLLABORATIVE RESEARCH IN INNOVATIVE FOOD

This case study investigates a public policy initiative for innovative food in a European country. This initiative ran between 1998 and 2008, through two subsequent research programmes, and leading to the set-up of several university-industry research centres within the food industry.

The following analysis is based upon written documents (including applications, annual reports and final reports) as well as interviews.

In total, 66 collaborative research projects were conducted. Firms co-finance these projects; they help set the agenda; and they expect future competitive benefits. All in all, 88 firms were involved including primarily large firms active in food processing in Europe and globally. They include dairy companies, food processing companies, packaging companies, national farmers' cooperatives and also a few academic spin-offs. The firms are quite diverse ranging from business units within global food companies to large farmers' cooperatives that process raw material into food (such as wheat into flour and pasta). Most companies were involved in only one project each, with only 28 firms being involved in more than one project. A few large global companies were, however, participating in many projects. The national farmers' cooperative was by far the most active company, involved in more than one-third of the projects.

Let us first and foremost point out that, in terms of benefits for the involved firms, it is clear that these research projects rarely lead directly to products and commercialization. Products were only reported as an outcome in five of the 66 examined projects.

The firms do not expect new products to result directly from the collaborative projects, but they instead expect to develop products in the long run or obtain other benefits. Indeed, the following discussion and illustrative examples indicate that even the direct impacts often involve fairly complex innovation processes inside the firms (especially in relation to their core products) and also outside the firm (in relation to their markets, sources of knowledge and so on).

In those projects that did directly result in products, however, the pay-off from investments in these projects seems to be considerable. Many participants from industry as well as universities and research institutes also expect that several of the projects they are involved in will bear more direct financial returns in the form of products in the years to come.

The case study shows that the expected and actual benefits of collaborative research include the development of firms' competencies per se and their products, but also more indirect benefits such as getting access to a stock of useful knowledge and skilled labour as well as networking and social interaction. Previous work (Laage-Hellman et al., 2009) developed a full-scale case analysis, which examined the research programmes' most important impacts on commercialization in the industry. The outcomes of the studied collaboration can be broadly categorized as follows:

- Prototype and product development
- New firms
- New practical methods, technologies and equipment
- Technology and knowledge transfer
- New networks.

The renewal of this traditional industry thus includes directly commercially viable outcomes, in the form of new products, new technologies and venture creations. The collaborative research thus lead to a direct impact on innovation, but mainly it leads to indirect outcomes that can provide inputs for later commercial development, such as developing and gaining access to networks or monitoring state-of-the-art developments in knowledge.

Clearly, companies can participate in these types of collaborative projects in different ways, and to different extents. Therefore, the indirect and direct benefits that companies gain from these projects are related to their level of engagement and interest. In practice, the firms engaged in these research programmes in different ways, ranging from providing funding for university-industry research centres, to devoting some time of employees to projects, to providing academic researchers with access to equipment and instrumentation and so on. This illustrates how KIE in the broad sense involves many actors in society, as they translate knowledge into competitiveness.

Below, we present short examples illustrating the benefits found within each of the above-mentioned outcome categories. Many of the projects are related to corporate entrepreneurship – that is, innovative outcomes for established firms – although there are also academic spin-offs involved in the research programmes and a few examples of venture creation. In particular, the examples illustrate how these benefits aid companies to improve their competitiveness, and hence how the projects are part of renewing the industry.

12.2.1 Prototype and Product Development

The firms conceptualize innovation as involving complex processes, which are mainly inside firms. In their perspective, this involves prototypes and product development, which will later result in actual products and services.

Of the 66 projects, 17 report prototype and products development as results from the collaborative research. The actual product development, or final product, was not considered a joint effort. Rather the projects provided the groundwork for it, and thereafter the companies completed the actual product development as an internal affair. The following statement by a firm involved in collaborative research projects can help specify the overall relationship between collaborative research and internal company development for the large firms:

> That is the way it is, you are in the project, sometimes with competitors, you learn and then you take the knowledge back home and try to translate it. And once in product development on our own, we cannot be that open about it anymore, we do not just call the researcher for help on specific problems. At that stage, the project has become a company-internal and secret project.

Much of the actual product development thus occurs inside the boundaries of the large firm, and usually under conditions of secrecy in order to protect their own appropriability regime.

A research project, which aimed to develop consistency-optimized food for health and well-being in the elderly, illustrates that while commercialization of the research results will take place in a large firm the development required inputs from many others. Thus, in this example many stakeholders were involved in developing a new product line, or at least provided the base for the participating firm to develop it. This is why this project involved not only the product developing company but also key suppliers and end-users, in the form of elderly care takers. The results in terms of learning can be said to understand how and why certain types of consistency would be appropriate for the elderly. These were useful results not only for the product line (about 1 per cent of the firm's turnover in 2008 with expectations for future growth) but also the firm's whole special foods unit. It has acquired useful knowledge about the elderly and published articles in peer-reviewed journals together with academic researchers. The latter is very useful especially for selling in export markets. In this example, the company clearly took over the responsibility for product development, and it has expectations for the future.

Another example dealing with a large dairy firm illustrates how product development can be more of an unplanned result from two different projects. This firm participated in two projects that were thematically somewhat similar, but involved collaborations with two separate research groups, at two different points in time. In the first project, the idea of a potential product formed when discovering the effects of certain bacterial properties upon fermentation. The second project, together with a human intervention study outside the project, largely confirmed the knowledge and ideas from the former project. Based on these results in combination with internal competencies, the company created an in-house development project. Still, they felt that they could rely on one of the research groups with which they have kept close contacts over many years. This includes continued interaction both with the researchers and their students.

Interestingly enough, in this illustrative example from the dairy industry, the company was not sure if the academic researchers would understand the link between the research project and product development. 'If you ask the researchers in the two projects, they may not see our product as a direct consequence of the projects, but for us it was.'

About two years after the dairy company started its own development work, the product is on the market and a significant turnover in the first year is expected. In addition, the two projects have together provided the firm with knowledge and ideas that they believe they can translate into even more products: 'We have only just begun to scratch the surface of this area.'

It is well known that the time lag between idea and commercialization may be many years. We can provide an illustrative example, where the commercial potential was discovered at a fairly early stage, but the actual product development has taken a long time. Commercialization is coming closer 10 to 15 years after the emergence of the original idea, which was developed in a smaller project outside the public policy programmes studied here.

The researchers behind this project patented their discovery and set up a KIE venture around the patent in order to commercialize it. However, the timing was bad – just after the dot.com crash. Therefore, it was difficult to raise money and after a few years of struggling, the patent rights were sold to a larger food company.

However, this company has not yet succeeded in developing a final product. It did participate in the collaborative research, especially working with two PhD students on sensory aspects such as taste, aroma and consistency. The company has also been focusing on rollouts of other products, where it already had possession of the rights. The company still sees a great market potential for a coming product, domestically as well as internationally, and this benefit will come irrespective of whether they produce it themselves or license production to other producers. This example also illustrates that ideas initially developed in KIE ventures can be sold to and developed by large companies, even if the original KIE venture does not succeed by itself.

12.2.2 New KIE Firms

Two projects reported that they were involved in venture creation. One resulted in a new firm, and the other resulted in a new centre, which was incorporated as a firm.

The first KIE venture started from one early research project. The project developed an online measurement method based on microwave technology for detection of foreign bodies in food. The original idea was conceived in 1997, in an earlier project with a dairy firm in another European country. The KIE venture was started in 2004. However, the idea needed further development and a research project was therefore started involving a national institute for food and agricultural research and an institute of technology. The firm is a spin-off from the national institute. According to the founder, the public funding for the innovative food centre was very important as it provided financing for the early phases of development, and led to a patent. In 2006, the company was awarded further funding through a national programme, oriented towards research intensive small companies. In 2007, the KIE had five employees and a turnover of three million euros.

As our second example shows, KIE ventures may be founded with overlapping public and private funding and research objectives. This KIE venture resulted from a project designed to support a research centre that could do tests for industry of the health effects of food. Hence, the project objective was to create a new university centre that industry could use for testing purposes.

Researchers at the university had developed the methodology and technology needed to make the tests. They then started to receive requests from industry to perform such tests, but they were not so interested in doing tests per se, as this was time-consuming and not always clearly related to the research objectives. The researchers there-fore saw the establishment of a centre oriented towards industrial needs as useful.

This centre was started around 2003, and financed primarily from national public policy, especially during the first three years. This support was very important and beneficial as it worked as 'a catalyst, or rather, as a venture capitalist apart from that they did not take any ownership in the center'. During a build-up period, the centre also received support from two universities through the collaborative research, and from regional and national public agencies. Moreover, the national regulatory agency served as an adviser to the project. In this period, the centre already had several national as well as international clients. In 2008, the centre became an independent shareholding company, and afterwards this new venture has succeeded fairly well – it is profitable and continues to grow in terms of employment. There is also a continuous bilateral exchange between this venture and university departments. Hence, this KIE venture is incorporated as a firm, but its main orientation is to diffuse the technique to industry.

12.2.3 New Practical Method, Technologies and Equipment

Technology was an important outcome, in that 28 of the 66 studied projects reported that an important outcome were new practical methods, technologies and equipment. This outcome category covers many different aspects of relevance to industry. Most are related to practical methods that range from new, fast methods for quality assurance when frying in fast-food stands to new ways of preparing food. The pay-off time for these results varies with the aims of the projects.

For example, one project was run on self-contained factories in food, with the objective of reducing waste in dairy production. This project focused on new sensor and filtering techniques, and these were introduced in a large dairy firm in order to reduce unnecessary waste from the flows in the production. Improvements in such aspects are of interest to the whole production chain from farmers to dairy producers, and industrial participation therefore includes major equipment producers as well as a large dairy company. The project required, among other things, the development and testing of several new filtering methods. This development was conducted by PhD students together with production technicians at the dairy company. The results proved valuable to the dairy company as it learned, among other things, what membranes to use when filtering, how to wash them and also how to clean these fluids. These are procedural changes in knowledge, applied to the specific context of business. These technical developments and procedural changes thus reduced waste in production. This resulted in the technique being introduced at dairies and manufacturing plants.

A second illustrative research project also addressed methods, and its importance to industry, again from the dairy industry. This project aimed to investigate the health effects of functional foods. It addressed how probiotic bacteria influence the genes that regulate fat metabolism in the body, and includes much basic research, which was conducted together with university researchers and an academic spin-off. According to the dairy company, there are specific reasons why the relationship between the basic research and the methods are valuable to them:

The advantage of this project, even if there is much basic research, is that the techniques and methods can be applied to several biomarkers in parallel. This in turn enables us to relatively quickly find different applications that are then of interest within the company.

This project employed a new technique that was being developed, and one that was new to the participating firms. Taken together with the biomarkers research project, this new technique provided one way of mapping the effects of lactic acid bacteria in the body, something that was of great interest to the participating dairy firm.

This was primarily a basic research project, and many scientific results were achieved early on. The dairy company had worked within the area prior to the project, and could translate some of the results into aspects useful for the company, but they also recognize that commercialization and pay-off are uncertain and may come far in the future.

A final illustration of how research projects develop methods and techniques, which can be useful to industry, is a project on acrylamide. This project can be seen as a direct response to the alarm about acrylamide in food (in, for example, potato chips and bread) in 2002, and the project was established and running in parallel to a larger European Union project addressing the same issue.

This project was thus concerned with how to reduce acrylamide in bakery products, especially bread, and specifically how to develop methods that could reduce the amount of acrylamide that results from the bakery process. The project identified two methods that could reduce acrylamide. Some 20 companies were in the network and monitored the results.

None of the participating bakeries immediately implemented the new techniques. The explanations as to why this knowledge was not incorporated into industry were threefold. Firstly, debates at the World Health Organization (WHO) level were ongoing about the health effects of acrylamide and hence legislation did not yet require such changes to be made. Secondly, implementing in particular one of these specific methods required significant changes in production through capital investment. Thirdly, that the project was more of a preparatory project to increase understanding and awareness in case legislation would change.

From the perspective of industry, this project hence enabled companies to be prepared and learn more about these issues (rather than resulting in knowledge about methods to implement immediately into new production facilities).

12.2.4   Technology and Knowledge Transfer

Of the 66 research projects, 12 explicitly stated in their reports that technology transfer from university to industry was an important result. However, interviews with firms and researchers revealed that knowledge transfer was more common than these project reports suggest. Specific examples given relate to, for example, the transfer of knowledge on how to perform new methods of analysis, the transfer of a specific technology or general knowledge on what technologies actually exist and can be used by the involved firms.

A first illustrative example is about food safety, and addresses how multiple projects have been involved in transferring the knowledge of new analysis methods to the participating companies. One research group had several related projects, and these were all concerned with developing better and faster diagnostics and analysis in order to improve food safety. This development occurred continuously over time through roughly three stages. The first stage concerned identifying the presence of different organisms, the second stage determining the number of organisms in a sample and in the third stage they attempted to determine the activity of the organisms in the sample. This last stage is important as it may be used to see how, for example, natural additives inhibit or increase the virulence of organisms in food.

Particularly in this case, one of the participating firms that focuses its business in this area has benefited, as it has gained competence in knowledge, for example, molecular analysis of DNA. The knowledge transfer in this case was much facilitated by an industry PhD student, financed by the company and supervised at the university. However, upon project completion, some of the other larger food producers have also set up new platforms to utilize the analysis methods, thus benefiting from the knowledge transfer. Knowledge transfer occurred further through workshops and active firm involvement in the project, and helped educate industry. A similar but more general point was made by another researcher in this project, namely, that one important effect of the projects is to make the industry realize what techniques and competences actually exist within national boundaries.

One dairy firm started the projects with universities, as a way to avoid developing its own R&D capabilities. The firm had no research department, and was too small to set up the different projects by itself. The firm therefore relied extensively on these collaborations with universities. Pointing to the specific projects within the research programme, the firm regarded these to be very important, as they had exposed them to new knowledge in areas of interest for current and future development of functional food products, specifically about the relation between bacteria, fermentation and nutritional uptake. Moreover, the university researchers expressed that they learned about the practical aspects of the product development process, concerning, for example, what problems can arise in the scale-up of processes, and how long development can sometimes take.

Three firm representatives who have been involved in a large number of projects suggest that an important part of a successful transfer of knowledge in the project is the intensity of the joint activities. By intensity, they mean, for example, use of MSc and PhD student theses, the frequency and regularity of meetings and contacts, the engagement of industry and the use of workshops. A second view, given by a university researcher, stresses that where it is possible, the best way to ensure a transfer is to have projects that continuously deliver products. The researcher particularly stressed a demonstration project or technique, which can be set up in the firm's environment in order to make the project concrete and 'real' to the firm.

12.2.5 New Networks

About one-fifth of the projects (11 of 66) report the development and access to new networks, including researchers and firms, as a result of the collaborative research. Most pertain to new research networks, although the interviews suggest that more networks were created between companies than found in the written reports.

Networks mattered as a way to access resources and ideas before the collaborative research. In many instances, the partners had already collaborated in prior projects. Many interviewees said that they felt this is hardly surprising as 'you rarely apply for money for something which you don't know at all or have been into before'. As a consequence of the importance of previous competencies, many of the project constellations also have a long history. Often two main partners had worked together for many years, and then in the public policy initiative for innovative food, they extended their core relationships into a new, larger network.

Sometimes new networks were created, and these networks were regarded as useful by industry. One project of particular interest in this regard involved several dairy firms on hygiene issues. Although these firms were competitors, one result of the project was a lasting network among the participating firms as well as to other contacts of the research institute leading the project. The reason this worked out so well was that although the companies were competitors in terms of final products, this research project focused on hygiene issues that was a problem common to all companies: 'If one dairy company gets problems with hygiene, it does not only hit that company but all dairy firms collectively.' As a result of the project, this new network continued to exist, and its members continue to exchange knowledge about how to investigate different problems and how they can work with hygiene in production.

While projects may not always create networks that are maintained and used on a frequent basis, they do result in connections across the sectoral system of innovation that make it easier to get into contact with people, and access market knowledge. These connections are useful in other ways than direct commercialization:

> We don't use the connections we make to primarily call researchers for consultation on specific problems. But if we have a research question that we need feedback on, we know where to turn to, and we can also use these connections to get a hold of right people in, for example, advisory board functions.

These network linkages took different forms in different projects. Stated benefits to firms included information flow, similar to the above example, but also in other fields. The benefits are clear in the field of DNA analysis, because 'while we are many different actors, we all work with the same basic technology and face the same basic challenges, so by creating connections among us we can speed up the progress of our field'.

Finally, projects did not necessarily lead to the formation of new networks and continued collaboration. This contention is further supported by comments from the interviews that 'when you don't have a project with common resources, you don't keep much contact, unless you have a personal contact, or try to keep someone attached to your department through, for example, an unsalaried associate professorship'. Network creation was not found to be an 'automatic' process, but something that requires commitment and interests.

12.3 WHAT HAVE WE LEARNED?

The case study has answered the following two questions, in the context of renewal in a low-tech industry:

> In what ways can new scientific and technological knowledge help stimulate renewal of products and services in traditional low-tech industries like food?

What are the expected benefits to firms from participating in collaborative research?

By examining all 66 collaborative research projects from two subsequent public policy programmes within the food industry, we have provided a case study of how public policy initiative renewed the industry, in terms of mapping out the direct and indirect outcomes of these collaborative research projects. What we have learned is that, while the research programmes were designed to stimulate corporate entrepreneurship and KIE through collaboration, the projects rarely led directly to products and commercialization (through, for example, firm creation).

Collaborative research does lead to renewal, but it does so mainly through long-term development of competencies and indirect benefits. A few KIE ventures are developed and involved in this case study of collaborative research in innovative food, but in general the new knowledge and techniques are used by large companies in agriculture and food. The interactions lead to a building up of the future potential for innovations.

12.4 QUESTIONS FOR FURTHER REFLECTION

Is this form of collaborative research likely to be a good way to renew other types of low-tech industry? Why or why not?

Does society benefit when public money is spent on subsidizing the development costs of new areas, such as innovative food? Explain your reasoning.

If you plan to develop a KIE venture in the agriculture and food industry, how should the firm position itself, relative to the huge global players, relative to national firms and cooperatives, and relative to national regulation?

REFERENCES

Laage-Hellman, J., M. McKelvey and M. Johansson (2009), 'Analysis of chain-linked effects of public policy: effects on research and industry in Swedish life sciences within innovative food and medical technology', *VINNOVA Analysis*, 2009, 20.
Lundvall, B. and S. Borrás (2005), 'Science, technology and innovation policy', in J. Fagerberg, D. Mowery and R.R. Nelson (eds), *The Oxford Handbook of Innovation*, Oxford: Oxford University Press, pp. 599–631.

Mowery, D. and B.N. Sampat (2005), 'Universities in national innovation systems', in J. Fagerberg, D. Mowery and R.R. Nelson (eds), *The Oxford Handbook of Innovation*, Oxford: Oxford University Press, pp. 209–39.

13. Financing and privatizing a visionary research endeavour in proteonomics: the case of ProSci in Australia

Johan Brink and Maureen McKelvey

13.1 INTRODUCTION

This chapter describes the story of ProSci, which is a visionary research endeavour in protein science, or proteonomics. The knowledge intensive entrepreneurship (KIE) venture starts with individual scientists at a research group at an Australian university, and then moves to become a life science company, but the story does not end there. After years of efforts to turn the public research endeavour into a private venture, the financial situation forces most of the participating researchers to return to the public sphere as university senior scientists.

During the decades analysed in this case, the venture has gone through an almost explosive development, involving both ups and downs and shifting organizational forms. The case study primarily covers issues related to financing and privatizing research and technologies within the life sciences and biotechnology. This chapter addresses the close linkages between how the firm can use public and private financing to act upon innovative opportunities as well as the complex impacts that founders – but also other financiers like venture capitalists – can exert upon the later phase of venture management and development.

The case study illustrates these issues, but the firm is also interesting in itself due to its advanced scientific and technological knowledge. ProSci has been involved in many efforts in the field of protein research and proteonomics. Among the different projects and technologies that they have undertaken, the most well known is their visionary development effort to create an integrated research instrument for large-scale protein research, called hereafter IRI. This company – and the individual scientists – have truly been at the international forefront of their fields for

close to two decades. This is perhaps why this case study can demonstrate some of the challenges of moving between the organizational forms
of university research group and academic spin-off. The company can be
said to represent a typical knowledge intensive entrepreneurial effort
within this particular industry. As an academic spin-off, it is based on the
entrepreneurial opportunities emerging in rapidly developing scientific
and technological fields, which the founders as academic researchers
helped to establish and develop. However, the story does not end with
these scientific and technological developments. In fact, commercial
development required major research and development effort over extensive periods of time, thus requiring significant investment and new
rounds of financing over many years.

In this case study, the investment and performance measures are
extremely volatile, mainly due to factors in the external environment but
also due to management decisions. The company must continue to access
new sources of financing, and decide between expansion and contraction
in different activities in the firm. That is why this case study can be used
to illustrate how the development of an academic spin-off is shaped by
new and different opportunities to finance its research activities. The firm
is initially created to take advantage of both the potential commercial and
financing opportunities in the emerging scientific field of protein science,
at a time when the financing milieu was very positive for starting KIE
ventures. However, as the industrial and financial milieu in the global life
science industry worsens, and as public policy shifts foci, their ability to
access new rounds of financing decreases. Still, for actors with cash, they
have the opportunity to grow the firm through mergers and acquisitions,
because other life science ventures end up in periods of financial distress.

The chapter addresses and illustrates the following questions:

> How did the researchers mobilize finance in order to realize their
> visions?
>
> How did this affect long-term relationships between the university
> and the KIE venture?
>
> How is firm development related to the shifting financial milieu, the
> strategy of the entrepreneurs and the rapid development of know-
> ledge and technologies?
>
> Why did the commercialization require such huge investments?
> What were the effects upon their research of obtaining different
> types of financing from public and private sources?

13.2 FINANCING KNOWLEDGE DEVELOPMENT

This KIE venture started as an academic spin-off. Coming together at the end of 1998, a small group of senior researchers put together their letters of resignation from the university. This would be the start of the roller coaster ride of ProSci, a science-based entrepreneurial venture which at times in the first years was said to represent Australia's next big thing – at least in the popular business press.

The opportunity identified for the KIE venture was based on rapid scientific developments, and the field around protein science was developing extremely quickly during the 1990s. Protein science was especially driven by the combined developments of three different technologies. Firstly, new analytical technologies in mass spectrometry (MS) such as electrospray ionization (ESI) and matrix-assisted laser desorption/ ionization (MALDI). Secondly, improvements in protein separation techniques, such as the immobilization of the pH gradient that reduced the problems with reproducibility separation in 2D Gel electrophoresis. Finally, the advancements of computing power, desktop computers and data communications networks reduced the cost of all-embracing research projects. As the public information about identified proteins grew, it was also easier to identify new proteins. Several databases emerged such as Protein Prospector (University of California, San Fransisco), ProFound (Rockefeller University) and Mascot (Matrix Science). There was now the possibility to analyse the composition of very large molecules, such as entire proteins.

The increased computing power and development of databases also implied that the complete analysis of the protein content in cells was becoming feasible at a reasonable cost and effort. By matching the results from the MS instruments with already known proteins in databases, the researchers could focus on the unique protein content in each sample. Taken together these techniques provided a simple method for finding differences in protein content between different cells, with implications for human health care. A sample from a patient would quickly reveal differences in the protein contents as compared to a control sample. Just the opposite, finding a strange protein in a cell could signal the potential association, or risk, of having a disease, creating biomarkers of diseases. The development in the early 1990s thus catalysed entirely new experimental approaches and opened up new types of biological questions to experimentation, resulting in the renewal of the field of protein research (Aebersold, 2003). The idea was raised of developing a protein mapping project, especially to identify the entire protein expression in different human cells and thereby create protein maps or atlases. All such efforts were greatly dependent on a fast, sensitive and reliable technique to identify the proteins once they were separated and isolated. Commercial protein research was thus dependent also on the associated development of research instruments.

13.2.1 Starting the Venture

The word proteome was first used in 1994. The term was defined as the protein complement of the genome, or the complete human DNA sequence, and the process of studying the proteome was thus called proteomics. One of the persons active in ProSci was Watkins, a PhD student, who had created the word some months earlier as he was struggling to finalize his PhD thesis. Watkins's supervisor was a well-known scientist in the protein science community. He had spent time at several top research institutes such as the Max Planck Institute and the University of Oxford. Just two years previously they had set up a new research group, taking advantage of the emerging opportunities in protein research and working closely with different research instrument manufacturers. Professor Richards had been working with external collaborating companies before and had during the later years been involved in a few less successful efforts to commercialize university-based research results. The research group was soon running a rather expansive research programme, involving several generations of postgraduate students – at one stage the group had up to 16 PhD students.

In order to effectively perform such a programme within this specific scientific field, they deemed that a rather big and diverse research group was necessary. Then in the mid-1990s the landscape for Australian research funding changed in that the Keating government (1991–96) came into power and reduced basic research funding during the recession.

The visionary idea was to further industrialize this special kind of protein research. Richards had seen the success of previous efforts by, among others, Craig Venture to industrialize genomic research. The goal was set to do the protein research in a more labour-efficient way, and to take part in the development of research equipment. The group successfully applied for and was awarded a major research grant at the end of 1995 and the development of the National Protein Centre (NPC) at the university started. The decision was political in that the NPC and other life science initiatives benefited at the expense of a major expenditure on the European Southern Observatory's very large telescope in Chile.

Despite these grants, it was increasingly difficult to fund the salaries and the ongoing research projects. The majority of grants were used for the construction of facilities, instruments and equipment.

In order to keep the group together, additional external sources of funding were necessary. Increasingly, the research group turned to work with a range of different private companies just to fund the ongoing research. These external partner firms engaged in relationships. These collaborations involved the development of instruments and technologies as well as protein research projects applying the developed instruments to targeting disease mechanisms, therapeutics or diagnostics.

By 1998, the research group put in a major research application for a Cooperative Research Centres' (CRC) programme, which was designed to increase interactions between university and industry. This application required co-financing from companies, and they had successfully negotiated these, as well as agreements with international instrumentation companies. However, their CRC grant application was turned down. The senior researchers were anxious to keep the group together.

The alternative of an academic spin-off seemed attractive. The idea of starting a KIE venture based on selling research services and developing proprietary integrated research instruments for protein research had been around for a while. 'In reality we had been running the group as a small firm anyhow.' They had also done some minor technological developments in relation to commercial partners, and the group thought the time was right for full commercial development of several technologies, which together formed the IRI platform.

A key issue was patents and intellectual assets, or intellectual property (IP). As part of the process of starting the venture, the research group began negotiating with the university, and offered equity in the venture in exchange for the transfer of IP for the previously developed technologies, research contracts and equipment. The university was positive but cautious and turned down this initial proposal. Around the same time, one of the external partner firms refused to finance a large research project at the university, due to their high overhead expenses.

ProSci was then started. The firm was 100 per cent owned by the six founders together with three businessmen from the city. The university, however, kept the ownership of all previously developed IP. In addition, several external firm partners maintained collaboration with the university, in effect splitting the researchers from the NPC into two groups – those who joined ProSci and those who remained at the university.

During this first year, ProSci bootstrapped its first year of existence by some collaborating companies providing equipment and others providing cash. With the university, in exchange for continuing supervision of former students and cash, ProSci obtained access to essential research equipment at the NPC centre.

13.2.2 Riding on the Wave of Technology Hype

ProSci was in the middle of an international hype about the technology. In the spring of the 2000, protein science came into the limelight of popular science. The Human Genome projects, with their draft map of all human genes, were approaching their completion. As scientists prepared to celebrate, attention turned to the next big thing – which was to understand what the genes do – the proteins. Celera Genomics Group, led by Craig Venture, announced its intention to enter the protein race: 'We are going to build the Celera proteomics facility. It's a major, major effort,' says Venter (*Businessweek*, 10 April 2000). The expectations about this emerging scientific field were extremely high. Funding for proteonomic projects included public research as well and pharmaceutical corporations such as Bayer, Merck and Pfizer started to enter proteomics projects.

For the newly created firm ProSci, this global hype and the expectations of protein science led to some changes. Because some years had passed, and the technologies had been dormant, the firm and the university could come to an agreement; ProSci took over the IP. For ProSci, the opportunity was to focus on the technology and develop this in external partnerships in order to minimize the capital requirements and still maintain ownership over the firm.

In 2000 this led to the first commercial collaboration devoted to the development of the IRI platform for protein research. Collaboration was initiated with an established Japanese equipment manufacturer, which the group had already been collaborating with back at NPC. During the autumn several other firm collaborations followed, which helped make ProSci a node for technological development. These collaborations also put an end to the peculiar relationship with the NPC, because now ProSci could access research instruments through their commercial partners. Together with the developed prototype for IRI, this opened up additional opportunities and expansion of contract research. Still, the public financing continued in some ways in that the project was co-funded by a government grant. In order to further fund these technological developments, the company then sold 10 per cent of the company in September 2000 with the help of a major investment bank. The largest investor was a state-owned investment fund – with the goal of driving technological and regional development through managing governmental wealth and state employee pension funds. The second largest investor was a publicly listed venture capital fund, a pooled development fund, which is a special investment fund created in Australia to promote investments in small- and medium-sized enterprises (SMEs) in exchange for tax exemptions.

13.2.3 Cash, Growth, Acquisitions and Visions

ProSci used their cash to grow through acquisitions and try to realize their visionary research endeavour. In late 2000, ProSci first used this newly raised money to acquire a small research and development group in the USA, which had been involved in similar integrative large-scale protein analysis equipment. The previous owner was a larger biotech firm, Genomics Solutions, which had to restructure due to financial difficulties in the shake-out from the dot.com bubble. ProSci went for this acquisition partly to strengthen their technological development project and also to increase market visibility in the US market, and to acquire some manufacturing capabilities. The expansive growth of ProSci continued the following year, 2001, when the group of design engineers who had been involved in the initial development of the first prototype was taken over. Later on, they took over a group of researchers within diagnostic applications from a local biotechnology firm. A third new business model hence emerged within the contract research unit to find proteins as biomarkers for diagnostic applications based on internal working with the IRI prototype.

The autumn of 2001 was full of additional expansion activities. A second private placement raised money from external investors valuing the company at over 300 million Australian dollars (AUD). In 2001 ProSci also entered yet another collaboration, this time with IBM, to be their official partner for the information technology (IT) system in the research instruments. In addition, ProSci entered a range of rather open and publicly funded research relationships using their internally developed IRI systems. For example, in August the company entered an agreement with the Buck Institute for Age Research in California in order to understand the mechanisms behind ageing, especially oxidative stress. The Buck institute, itself a non-profit research organization, in turn led a joint project with a small drug research firm developing therapeutic compounds.

The visions were realized initially. After three and a half years of operations, in mid-2002, the development of the IRI system was completed. ProSci had its first major sale in the form of a joint venture with a major contract research organization, Charles River's discovery and development facility in the USA. The deal was made and ProSci contributed with 20 per cent ownership – mostly in exchange for the instruments being delivered. 'It was in a form of joint venture, we didn't really want to do it, but we couldn't say no.' The new facility opened in April 2003 in order to offer fee-for service operations mostly in toxicology testing towards biotechnology and pharmaceutical firms. Another agreement was made in 2002 with C-Qentec Diagnostics, a subsidiary of Aventis Crop Science to improve its wheat quality diagnostic – based on the test from the research group taken over the year before. In 2003 ProSci sold another complete set-up of their system to Iberica Co., in collaboration with Kurume University in Japan. In the autumn of 2003 this was followed by the third sale of a complete IRI system – this time to the Forest Research Institute in Malaysia.

As a result of of the quick growth and technical development between 2000 and 2003, the firm received several awards, among theme 'Rookie of the Year Award' from IBM and Frost and Sullivan's award for Technology Innovations, for being a rapid growth company and pursuing excellent technology development. The company also was named as one of the fastest growing SMEs in *Business Review Weekly*, one of the most read Australian business magazines. The fame and fortune of ProSci finally made its mark on the world of business education when they were described in a *Harvard Business Review* case study – growing from just six employees to over 100 in a mere four years.

13.2.4 The Tidal Changes: More Finance, More Competitors and Long Lead Times

By 2003, competing technological solutions were offered by large incumbent companies such as GE. The fact that the university had held onto IP had slowed development as well. The early and rapid growth phase but slow sales was now followed by a tidal change.

One issue was that ProSci's management team became unsure about the market for IRI, their large-scale integrative technological solution. The sales team was now aware of the long lead times for sales of their system, and that the customers needed first to understand their needs and then raise the funds necessary for such huge investments in technology. For customers, this was a major issue when purchasing from a young firm without any established service and distribution channels. A decision was taken to increase the marketing effort: 'Having invested about 30 million AUD into developing technological products we needed to get serious, getting out selling it.' The vision was to manufacture and install 4–6 additional complete IRI platforms within the coming year. However, additional financing was necessary, and the solution was once again to turn to external investors. Yet, following this period of rapid growth, real problems started to emerge inside the company too. The amorphous growth in the previous two years, with several takeovers of already established groups, started to get out of control. ProSci made efforts to implement a new management structure by increasing traditional human resources (HR) practices, but did not pursue any real change within the business strategy. ProSci instead adopted a more conventional business structure, with project managers and different groups with clear responsibilities.

> The problem was that the two main businesses [technology development and contract research] started to develop in different directions, than the discovery group. The technology development had to go on, to be more commercialized, such as standardized, quality and so on. We had a functioning prototype which the discovery group used. The basic problem was that the discovery group needed fast, rapid and small modifications the whole time. That was too much for the technology group to handle; they needed to have longer time frames.

ProSCi had now grown to more than 100 employees, with an international research and sales office in the USA as well as Australia. ProSci had spent about 100 million AUD, of which 60 million AUD were from investors, 20 million AUD were from external partners and 20 million AUD were from sales, and yet a large share of the firm was still in the hands of the original founders. By mid-2003, ProSci was forced to seek additional financing in order to ramp up the marketing and sales effort but also the IRI system and software, and they chose the Australian stock exchange, ASX.

ProSci appointed a major investment bank, USB, with the intention of raising 50 million AUD. USB failed to gain significant interest from any institutional investors and by the autumn of 2003 another investment banker was hired. This time the strategy was first to find more experienced board members, and with the help of the two venture capital funds, two new well-known board members joined. Also Richards, the founding entrepreneur, was visible and worked to increase visibility and public relations (PR). When asked if his academic and research background sat uneasily with business, Richards replied that it made sense to go it alone and claim a stake in his ideas, and added regarding the financing situation: 'Frankly, it's a lot easier than writing grants to get government funding.' In principle, the research vision had not changed over the years, just the source of financing. In August 2004 a prospectus for raising an additional 20 million AUD was released, down from the initial idea of 50 million AUD the year before. However, this figure just matched the net operating cash flow as the company was running an annual negative result.

Almost immediately after the initial public offering (IPO), things started to change. On the 9 December 2004 the joint venture with Charles River was cancelled as this turned out to create a negative reputation round the effectiveness of IRI. A strategic review of the joint venture identified problems, with technologies related to the restructuring of yet another company in the life science industry. The new owners had different strategic intentions, so just eight days after the joint venture was cancelled ProSci signed an agreement to buy their pharmaceutical research partner firm Eukarion. Eukarion had during the autumn of 2004 been running out of cash, creating yet another opportunity for ProSci to acquire potential projects at a bargain price by just offering shares in venture and cash to continue running the different projects. The Eukarion group had a couple of promising drug development projects that were about to enter clinical trials. ProSci, with the new owners as well as the new board members, gradually realized the weak market demands for their IRI technological systems, and this forced a strategic revision.

> This has not been a stellar six months in terms of revenue. The CEO said he was hopeful that a number of sales to universities and research institutes would be finalized soon. We have not yet got pen to paper ... I'll be very disappointed if we don't start to see some real activity.

13.2.5 Crashed Visions and Turnaround Efforts

For ProSci, the years 2005 and 2006 involved significant changes. Not only had the punctured hype around protein science reduced any further abilities to raise capital, but also its former university, in the form of NPC, had started to compete in the market for research contracts and technological development with external partners. The market for IRI systems dropped as expectations on protein science dropped. Competing systems were emerging, and ProSci no longer had a first mover advantage. Around 2005 scepticism around the proteomics approach starts to appear in the main scientific journals.

> Our experience with serum marker screening tests has been terribly disappointing, and ... terribly costly in dollars and suffering for patients. [Our] perception [is] that the technology is unreliable.

To analyse the situation, they hired a well-known company turnaround specialist and former investment banker. As a result, the strategy of

ProSci once again drastically changed. A decision was made by the board to hire the turnaround specialist as a new Chief Executive Officer (CEO). As an outsider and new CEO, the turnaround specialist soon tried to change the culture from scientific to commercial and publicly announced his opinion:

> I found the most extraordinary bunch of assets managed in an equally extraordinary manner. The long-term opportunities for the business were not where the money was being spent. It was a flawed business plan. [Management in the biotech sector is 'as bad as it gets' as] they get so wedded to the science of the science and they forget the importance of the shareholders. I have heard of biotechs saying, 'We are not expected to make money.'

The original researchers and founders had lost control over their firm, and also their vision to develop IRI was no longer deemed fruitful.

The first change was to reduce the technological development effort significantly. This reduced the negative cash flow by more than 50 per cent, but also reduced the company to 60 employees, down from over 130 a year before. The second step was to cancel almost everything related to the further commercialization of the technological platform IRI. Instead ProSci focused upon the diagnostics and drug discovery business, through the identification of biomarkers. Several of these projects were based on external partner agreements with research funds or had come into the hands of ProSci through the previous opportunistic investments.

During the next years, as the technological development halted, the original entrepreneurial team left the firm. One became a systems biology professor, the second a director of a newly created centre, the third went to a private instrument company, the fourth back to the original NPC, with her several developed databases now open for public use, and finally Professor Richards became an independent investor and consultant in China.

At ProSci, after a mere two years, the turnaround specialist resigned. The medium-sized, high buzz firm with global ambitions that he had been recruited to was now downsized to 40 employees. Most development projects had been stopped, and only a few promising projects in the diagnostics area, all of them externally co-financed, had been emphasized. Stepping down, he handed over the role as CEO to Larry, the last of the founding partners. For Larry one of his first actions was to change the name of the company to signal a break with the past and highlight the new strategies in diagnostics.

Over the past few years, the management team has focused on leveraging the Company's core strengths in the validation and development of biomarkers and diagnostic tests. The divestiture of the technology platform and an exit from the therapeutic business enabled the allocation of the appropriate resources to achieve corporate growth. This fundamental shift in strategy has prompted the name change, and we are pleased to have the support of our shareholders.

One of the first actions was to out-license the IP rights of the therapeutic portfolio back to the original inventors, who simultaneously left the renamed company. After just three additional years with the new strategy, the co-financed diagnostic research projects were all wound up, most with an unsatisfactory result and the firm closed the remaining research efforts down.

13.3 WHAT HAVE WE LEARNED?

This case study has focused on the development of ProSci. It is an Australian KIE firm based upon the rapid advances in protein sciences, involving long-term networks with the university as well as firms in various industries but especially biotechnology and pharmaceuticals.

The first question posed was how the researchers mobilized financing for their visionary research endeavour in proteomics, and the impacts on the relationship with the university.

The initial entrepreneurial effort was not driven by profit motivations, but by the intention of the senior university scientists to keep the group together, in order to realize their very ambitious research visions. One reason to move from the university to a KIE venture was that the opportunities for private financing around 2000 seemed higher than the traditional public sources that finance through public sources and research grants. However, there was also a push, in that research application failed to attract financing, at the same time that an important collaborating business partner refused to pay the high university over-heads. Taken together, this finally convinced the researchers to start the venture.

An interesting issue is why the external environment was favourable to KIE ventures, in such a way as to help explain the ease of private financing in Australia and in this industry at that time. One reason is that biotechnology in general but especially these technologies created hype. Several similar technological ventures were created globally at the same time. Another reason was that in Australia, a key aim of public policy at the time was to push researchers to start academic spin-offs, and thus commercialize public knowledge. Several policy instruments facilitated these efforts. The major source of external financing came from either a newly created governmental venture capital effort in life sciences or through the listed SME investment fund delaying the tax deductions. Moreover, technical projects were supported by governmental development grants to companies, and for which public researchers were not eligible. Already most joint research projects were being done in collaboration with industry or else supported with non-profit organizations relying on charity and the benevolence of wealthy investors such as the Bill and Melinda Gates Foundation.

This early history of financing had longer term implications for the KIE venture, which were also relevant for obtaining additional financing. The ease of getting cash in the early days led to extensive growth and several opportunistic takeovers of companies globally. These takeovers later became the main areas for continued technical and product development, and the company put much less effort into the original vision around IRI. The IPO generated low interest from institutional investors, despite ProSci being well known in the popular business press. Publicity was partially due to active participation and PR activities and partially through heavyweight collaborations, such as with IBM, that ProSci could enter due to their technology IRI.

The second question addresses how choices of the firm are related to the shifting financial milieu, the strategy of the entrepreneurs and the rapid development of knowledge and technologies. This has to do with the development and management phase.

The case of ProSci describes the ongoing and multifaceted relationship between the entrepreneurial efforts and the university from which the firm once originated. Over time the firm and the university act both as competitors, customers and collaborators.

The case of ProSci highlights the important role that financing opportunities have in order to direct technological and scientific development in the interface between private and public research investments. The case of ProSci also emphasizes the increasingly blurred boundaries between open/public and closed/private knowledge-based entrepreneurship. The case study especially raises questions for discussion about how and why researchers strive to realize their visions, with the help of accessing different sources of financing and capital, while also de-emphasizing the strict gap thought to exist between private and public financing

The shifting financial milieu in the life science industry thus not only affected the growth process of this KIE venture but also shaped the development of knowledge strategies of individual researchers and the ability to finance their visions, and thereby the social value of knowledge originally produced in open, university-based, settings.

The final questions are: Why did the commercialization require such huge investments? What were the effects upon their research of obtaining different types of financing from public and private sources? In this case, it is obvious that there are close linkages between further development of scientific and technological knowledge and the development and management of the KIE venture. KIE in biotechnology and the life sciences is based and rooted in the long history of science development, across multiple fields.

The emerging vision of the original entrepreneurs was to construct an instrument, IRI, in order to map human proteins, and this idea could be found more than 20 years earlier. However, breakthroughs in three different bottleneck technologies (MS, Separation and computers) made the vision feasible by the mid-1990s. The original founder team as academic scientists were collectively well positioned to know the development in all three fields. In addition, they had previous experience of entrepreneurial activities. The relationships developed in the first years of NPC and during the CRC application constructed the initial relationships from which the business of ProSci was built. The firm did thus not build its portfolio of relationships from scratch but were a result of a decade long development endeavour within the university in which both knowledge, technologies, IP and relations had evolved.

These relationships and developed technologies gave ProSci a technological lead, and helped to establish the venture as a node, attracting several additional heavyweight collaborations, which is essential in the life science industry (Powell et al., 1996). However, despite this early lead ProSci failed to profit from its developed technology. This has been found in several cases of new technologies and a well-known difficulty for KIE (Teece, 1986).

Partial explanations for the difficulties of ProSci can be found in many related specifics of the case. One issue was the prolonged times for technical development and the need to purchase a complete system. One delay was because the university obstructed development of technologies by claiming ownership of previous developed IP. Because the technical characteristic of IRI was to be a complete system, this required lumpy investments to purchase the whole system. Moreover, this idea of selling a complete IRI system also reduced the researchers' ability to freely combine different instruments and equipment in a unique way – seen also in the internal drug and discovery projects within ProSci. Together with an unknown brand and the absence of a service network and distribution and organization compared to incumbent instrument manufacturers, these drawbacks partially explain the slow adoption of IRI by customers.

ProSci competed, if not explicitly, with the university-based scientists for research projects; both in terms of applying research technology in research service agreements but also as a technology development partner. Although never a goal in itself, to become a service provider was something ProSci initially did to cover its costs. As the NPC stepped up its activities, ProSci increasingly focused its accumulated financial resources on diagnostics, which is a product with an intermediate to short time to market.

ProSci refrained from the competitive and immediate service contract market and also ceased to invest in long horizon projects such as therapeutics and sales of IRI because they required an extensive sales and distribution organization with a reputation for reliability. With the help of profit motivated investments, ProSci actively contributed to the public open science development. Partially this occurred through the development of publications written by the joint research projects, motivated by publicity and increased legitimacy of IRI. In addition, several of the funding researchers, as well as other employees, went back to the university after doing research at ProSci. Some even took data and relationships developed at ProSci with them, turning them into assets of public research rather than private.

Finally, the volatility inside the firm is closely tied to financing and opportunities, and analysing this case therefore also has implications for evaluating performance and output. One aspect is naturally that the indicators that can be used are affected, including the traditional measures of entrepreneurial development such as firm size, growth and turnover. The fluctuation of these indicators can be used to consider what 'success' and 'growth' really mean in this context, over a number of years. Another aspect is that the shifts in financing – in this case of rapid knowledge development – have also caused profound changes in the direction of knowledge development, and by that we mean choices about which technologies to further develop and emphasize as important. This raises interesting questions about how scientific and technological knowledge are affected by market and business knowledge during the development and management phase of a KIE venture.

13.4 QUESTIONS FOR FURTHER REFLECTION

The ability to attract finance is pivotal for the development of KIE firms, and especially for firms with investments in the development of new products or technologies. Two key concepts that differentiate KIE ventures are their business cycle and the industry. How do you think entry rates may differ over the business cycle for academic spin-offs? Does ability to attract financing vary over industries, and why or why not?

Why did this small KIE venture fail to successfully commercialize the new technology (IRI) despite their technological superiority and early lead? What mistakes or key decisions would you recommend doing differently?

Apply this thinking to another research field in science and engineering. Can you identify how, why and when different types of actors, such as private, profit motivated firms and public actors (universities or research institutes), are involved in financing scientific and technological knowledge. Are they competing or collaborating?

REFERENCES

Aebersold, R. (2003), 'A mass spectrometric journey into protein and proteome research', *Journal of American Society for Mass Spectrometry*, **14**, 685–95.
Powell, W.W., K.W. Koput and L. Smith-Doerr (1996), 'Interorganizational collaboration and the locus of innovation: networks of learning in biotechnology', *Administrative Science Quarterly*, **41**, 116–45.
Teece, D. (1986), 'Profiting from technological innovation', *Research Policy*, **15**, 285–305.

14. Business models in Big Data in China: designing new opportunities through sequencing and bioinformatics

Yanmei Zhu and Maureen McKelvey

14.1 INTRODUCTION

This case study addresses Big Data, and especially how and why a knowledge intensive entrepreneurship (KIE) venture in China is developing its business model in sequencing and bioinformatics. The case is particularly interesting, partly for being in China, and also because of the unclear and evolving boundaries between public and private and between basic science and technology. The focus is upon designing opportunities, and especially how the firm takes decisions, and designs strategies, to exploit scientific and technological opportunities afforded by sequencing and bioinformatics, as applied to human health care.

The concept of the 'business model' refers to how firms do business – how they compete and make profits by using their competencies and resources to sell goods and services in the market. Firms, in other words, do business by combining internal resources to offer goods and services that add value to specific groups of customers (Magretta, 2002). The organization studied here is not only a firm, but the business model idea helps us understand the foci and organization of Big Data.

Drucker (1994) provided an early and influential definition of a business model. He defined a business model as follows: what an organization is paid for, what an organization considers to be meaningful results (how to make a difference) and where an organization must excel in order to maintain leadership. This definition is broad but useful. It is broad in that it relates to how the organization itself perceives the internal core assets, as well as how it reacts to customers and 'the market' value of the goods and services offered. The definition is useful in that it focuses attention upon how and why the firm can combine its internal assets in such a way as to compete in a market and how to survive within the institutional context.

Another way of stating this is that the 'business model' concept is used here in order to help us specify how and why the KIE venture may take advantage of business opportunities, as expressed in terms of strategies for collaboration and internationalization. The firm reacts to business opportunities by combining internal resources to offer goods and services that add value to specific groups of customers (including public ones), and this helps differentiate the firm from its competitors.

Big Data is a KIE venture, and has a shifting organizational form between company and research institute. The venture thus shifts between different organizational forms like a research institute and a firm over time, and this is partly due to demands placed by changes in scientific research and in the prospects of financing and markets. What is particularly interesting is why the venture had spent so much money on basic research, but at the same time shifted to more private market terms. In this case, it means that the firm can apply their research results in practical areas and then obtain profit to support their ongoing research and technological infrastructure. Becoming more market oriented also means that the firm can access leading research institutes in other countries and are able to publish in leading international journals.

This case study represents a fairly unique case, due to Big Data's participation in the international Human Genome Project in the 2000s as the only site from an emerging economy and due to their ambitious strategies.[1] Indeed, one of the reasons that this case study is interesting is its role as an extreme case of how quickly a venture from an emerging market can enter the world frontline. Moreover, this KIE venture also demonstrates the sometimes unclear boundaries between 'science' and 'commercialization' and between 'public' and 'private' in fields related to biotechnology and life sciences, which holds globally.

There may be aspects of this case that may be seen as unique to the China context, such as the role of the government and the ability of the KIE venture to access finance and capital. In this case, the government support – at national and regional levels – does help the company become more successful on the world market as a public-private hybrid organization.

Underlying the rapid emergence of Chinese KIEs on the global stage is also, in part, a result of national strategy and context. The Chinese national strategy of transforming itself from a manufacturing-oriented society to a knowledge-driven economy is an initiative dubbed from 'Made in China' to 'Innovated in China'.

China will spend $300 billion on science and technology, making biotechnology a major priority, in the years up to 2020. The Chinese government will work to further combine biotechnology with economic development and improve ordinary peoples' livelihood. The case company is also involved in, and has the ability to take the initiative, or co-initiative, in big global projects like the International Rice Genome Sequence Program (IRGSP) and the International HapMap Project.

This chapter focuses upon the rapid emergence of a KIE venture from China, based upon instruments and how they can exploit the scientific and technological push for sequencing and bioinformatics.

The KIE venture is analysed here in terms of developing their business model and how to act upon the opportunities afforded by genomics, as it impacts medical science and health care. This impact has also extended in more recent times to agriculture and food, although only mentioned in passing. The case study addresses the following questions:

> How does the KIE venture try to take advantage of the new business opportunities in health care, which are related to sequencing and bioinformatics?

> Over time, in what ways has the KIE venture developed its strategies and capabilities, including issues like collaboration, internationalization and reputation?

> What type of business models are currently being developed in an area with unclear boundaries between public and private and between basic science and technology?

14.2 THE KIE VENTURE AND OPPORTUNITIES IN HUMAN HEALTH CARE

This case study is of a Chinese venture, which is outspokenly focused upon a business model organized around the 'science and technology push' in areas of genetic sequencing and bioinformatics, although the firm is also affected by the dynamics of basic science and the market. This section initially addresses the first two questions, by presenting the case of Big Data chronologically. It does so while describing issues related to strategy for collaboration and internationalization together with the human resources and reputation. The third question on business models is then discussed.

14.2.1   Business Models and Opportunities in Genetic Sequencing and Bioinformatics

This area of human health care relies on large amounts of data. In terms of opportunities for new business models, it is clear that there is a scale effect, where very large investments are necessary to purchase and run the equipment, but there is a question about the competitive edge because simultaneously per unit costs are rapidly decreasing.

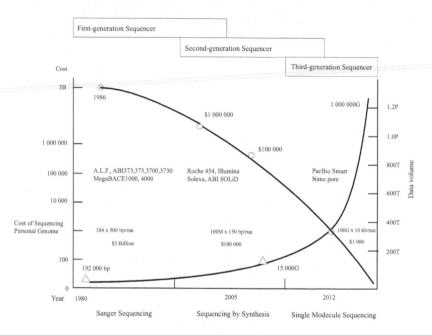

Figure 14.1   The cost and speed of sequencing

The science and technology push as the source of the opportunities can be illustrated by the graph in Figure 14.1.

Figure 14.1 demonstrates these radical shifts. Over the last three decades, enormous advances have been made in the technologies available for sequencing DNA, allowing increasing automation and higher throughput. Meanwhile, the sequencing cost dramatically declines from $3 billion for a human genome 20 years ago to approaching $1000 by 2012. The DNA sequencing technologies are divided into three generations: first-generation or Sanger sequencing (from the 1970s); second- or 'next generation' massively parallel sequencing (current); and third- or 'next-generation' sequencing (future).

Pressures on cost as well as the availability of large-scale data are relevant to the story as well. The bioinformatics and computational biology market is particularly booming in China and India, especially along with the dramatic decline of the sequencing costs. That plays to Big Data's strength, which is the integration of both the sequencing and the bioinformatics.

14.2.2 1999 to 2006: Founding Phase and Research Institute

China has actively worked towards developing the health biotechnology innovation system through public policy (Li et al., 2004). It was the only developing country to participate in the Human Genome Project (HGP). Specific subfields have been targeted, including therapeutic antibodies, severe acquired respiratory syndrome (SARS), gene therapy, functional genomics and stem cells.

Big Data was created in 1999. Initially it participated in the HGP as China's representative. Their goal was to take on 1 per cent of the human genome, and they achieved this under the international HGP (Nature, 2010). Their ambition from the beginning has been high and internationally oriented, aiming to lead in their field of sequencing and bioinformatics. Big Data was initially a pure research institute.

Moreover, in relation to the HGP, the Chinese Academy of Sciences (CAS) set up the Chinese National Human Genome Center based on Big Data. But after a time, there was serious conflict between CAS and Big Data. CAS institutes have an academic structure, with senior scientists often heading small teams, but Big Data had a different vision. They were building a large-scale sequencing operation staffed with an army of programmers and bioinformatics personnel because they forecast that the age of mass data would come in the near future when the value of gene data would be immeasurable. Moreover, there was little recognition of the importance of sequencing by the scientific community in CAS.

After the HGP was completed, Big Data shifted to a more general focus upon genomics, and they partnered with scientists. They primarily hired programmers and bioinformatics personnel in order to better analyse and work with the data generated through the genomics. Therefore, in this way, they could also offer specialized knowledge, as compared to partners who were experts in the science of specific therapeutic areas/diseases and agricultural areas.

Big Data moved to Hangzhou (Zhejiang Province in China) in exchange for funding from the local government. The rice genome was sequenced in 2002 and became a cover story in the journal *Science*. They were also able to quickly sequence several strains of SARS virus in 2003 (and enterohaemorrhagic *Escherichia coli* (EHEC) in Germany in 2011), leading to an increase in visibility and reputation. Later the first Asian genome was sequenced.

Success in this period was related to both obtaining partners and publishing prestigious basic scientific papers in areas like chicken, silkworm and panda genomics. They began to work with international scientific partners, and claim that their strategy has been, and remains, 'to drive down costs, increase speed and cover expenses' (Science, 2012).

14.2.3 2007 to 2012: Expansion and Venture

In 2007, Big Data relocated their headquarters to Shenzhen and founded the private, non-profit research institute, with a corresponding change in organizational structure towards a more hybrid one between the research institute and a commercial venture given their loss of financial support as a public research institute.

The move to Shenzhen Special Economic Zones, the window to China's reformation and opening up, was mainly due to their tolerance by this immigration city and recognition by local government officials. They were awarded ten million Renminbi as a start-up as well as 20 million Renminbi in annual grants (from the local government). They obtained a one billion Renminbi loan from the China Development Bank in 2010, due to the significance of the strategic and emerging biotechnology industry, on which they only pay interest for ten years before starting to pay back the principle. They will continue as a research institute, but also have private non-profit institutes in Hong Kong, Europe and the USA, as well as owning private companies for sequencing and clinical services.

In 2010, Big Data dramatically expanded its sequencing capacity in order to realize an ambition to sequence genomics at 'twice the speed and half the price' of anyone else. Globally, the costs are dropping dramatically, not only at Big Data but also for competitors. Moreover, Big Data has primarily employed their workforce in China, where wages are lower and highly competitive.

At the same time, they recently decided to open centres in Hong Kong, Europe and the USA, despite higher costs. There were two main reasons for this – one is to become or be perceived as key partners, reliable and so on by scientists around the world. The other is to be able to potentially tap into local sources of funding from national grants and foundations in these regions.

The integration of genomics and bioinformatics is the key to understanding Big Data's strategy and development in the business model. They used integration and internationalization, and have found that internal competencies and human resources are very important. They have continued to hire programmers and bioinformatics personnel, and rapidly expanded the workforce from dozens in 2007 to 3800 individuals in 2011. Their strategy is to develop massive sequencing capacity, and they used much of the bank loan to purchase more than 100 state-of-the-art sequencing machines from the US firm Illumina, based in San Diego. The purchases not only represent a stunning investment of at least $60 million in this cutting-edge technology, but also give them nearly twice the number of instruments as the largest sequencing centre in the USA, the Broad Institute at the Massachusetts Institute of Technology (MIT).

Big Data has had to develop capabilities and hire human resources in bioinformatics as well as in sequencing and genomics, due to the huge amount of data involved. These fields are intertwined in the science and the relevance usability of the data. Moreover, for disease-related genomics, 'you need to know how many samples and to what depth you have to sequence to maximize the statistical power to identify a particular gene or loci that is associated with a disease' (Science, 2012, p. 519). This requires additional knowledge in simulations and statistical models. Hence, the development of internal capacities in knowledge through hiring has been a key aspect of the development of the company and its focus.

Big Data also launched the 1000 Plant & Animal reference genomes project in 2010, and called for collaboration from around the world. The goal of the project is to generate reference genomes for 1000 economically and scientifically important plant and animal species. Therefore, by the end of 2011, the completed projects have included rice, silkworm, cucumber, panda, camel, oyster, ant, grouper, goose, crested ibis, potato genomes and more. Many other genomes are in the process of active sequencing.

By 2012, they were also working with other organizations on a large scale. The Chinese national gene bank in Shenzhen, initiated and operated by Big Data, has collected 13 PB (1 million GB) bio data, including genomes, transcriptomes, proteomes and so on, and about 400 000 biological tissue samples. This is an outstanding amount of data. We would have to watch for 40 000 years if the gene bank were to be viewed as a high definition (HD) movie, as a 1.5 hour HD movie corresponds to about 4 GB. The founding partner of Big Data said, 'We have a dream to sequence every living thing on Earth, to sequence everyone on Earth.'

With a group of cooperation partners including the Karolinska Institute in Stockholm, Big Data will sequence thousands of crops, animals and insects – and in humans plans to unravel the genomics of Mendelian diseases and pave the way for personalized medicine. For now, its bold ambitions are carrying the day. 'They make you realize the sky is the limit,' says Lennart Hammarström, at immunologist of the Karolinska Institute.

But Big Data has not only sequencing 'muscle', they also have an analysing 'brain'. Bio-IT World's Best Practices Awards Programme, which was established in 2003, recognizes organizations for their outstanding innovations and excellence in the use of technologies, practices and novel business strategies that will advance drug discovery, development, biomedical research and clinical trials. Big Data, the world's largest genomics organization, was honoured with the award in 2012 for their flexible green cloud computing infrastructure for de novo assembly and resequencing analysis.

14.2.4   Financing Activities that Link Basic Science and Applied Technology

Moreover, up until April 2012, they have published 50 academic papers in top-level journals including *Nature, Science, Cell* and the *New England Journal of Medicine* (NEJM). Nature Publishing Group published Nature Publishing Index (NPI) 2010 China. Big Data is ranked fourth of the top ten institutions in the index, just after CAS, the University of Science and Technology of China, Tsinghua University and Hong Kong University of Science and Technology (HKUST). Therefore, due to the contribution of Big Data, Shenzhen is ranked sixth of the top ten Chinese cities for high-quality basic research before Hangzhou, Guangzhou and Tianjin, where many universities and research institutes are located. Moreover, some authors of those high-quality papers have no PhD degrees. This is somewhat ironic, and perhaps even disturbing to most of the Chinese universities, especially when they are currently enthusiastic about publishing papers in Science Citation Index/ Engineering Index (SCI/EI) journals (Yanmei, 2012).

Big Data is also challenging a 'longba' in China, where basic research and industry are often separated. It seems very hard to integrate them. In 2011, 90 per cent of revenue came from sequencing and data services from scientific partners and health services from hospitals. This provides the financial support for their basic research.

According to the report 'China: the life science leader of 2020' from Monitor (Baeder and Zielenziger, 2011), 'China's sequencing power has the potential to tip the balance in innovation, the inventions and ideas that currently underlie the success of U.S. biotechnology,' argues Dr Jeanne F. Loring, a renowned stem cell researcher who is now director of the

Center for Regenerative Medicine at the Scripps Research Institute, writing in the journal *Science Progress*. 'China's investment in sequencing will allow the country to build a valuable intellectual property portfolio because new discoveries will be made at a furious pace,' she continued, noting that the emerging field of epigenetics – which can help determine how 'switches' in cells can be turned on or off – will demand more intensive sequencing and computer resources than mere genome sequencing. Already the home of the world's largest supercomputer, China is rapidly building the infrastructure to support integrated computational biology on a massive scale.

'Genomics revolutionized the life sciences,' says Jian Wang, president of BGI. 'But the growing flood of genomic data poses an enormous challenge to optimizing and sustaining the benefit of high-throughput sequencing technologies. They have made significant efforts to tackle this challenge to advancing life science research, and this cooperative agreement should provide an example for researchers worldwide on the importance and value of shared, sustainable data management and data manipulation in biological and medical studies.' Big Data has already made some significant moves on the genomics big data front. Last year, they launched their BGI-BOX cloud computing terminal server, which aims to allow non-bioinformatics experts to take advantage of genomic data sets and software analysis tools in their own laboratories. Jointly, BGI and BioMed Central launched *GigaScience*, a database and journal focused on hosting and publishing large-scale data.

Massive sequencing capacity is one prong of Big Data's strategy. It has also strived to blaze a trail in bioinformatics by developing free software for the community. They have been pursuing an open strategy in the whole effort. Bioinformatics has become increasingly important as the sequencing volume has grown.

14.2.5   Business Models in Health Care

This subsection covers the concept of business models in this KIE venture, and particularly how they are developing new opportunities in human health care, which arise due to Personalized or P4 medicine. We first outline the general opportunities opening up, then focus upon the differing types of demands, the various customers and the competitors. This subsection provides an answer to the third question.

McKelvey (2008) argues that the existing two dominant models are being challenged, due to serious problems of profitability, changing technologies and medical knowledge and changing demand. Moreover, she outlined a number of alternative business models; these are emerging due to P4 medicine. It is in this context that we should understand the development of the business model of this KIE venture, at the boundaries of public and private as well as of basic science and technology.

Human health care, biotechnology and pharmaceuticals represent major industries, but the products and services in industries related to human health face a change due to P4, medicine.

There is a need within health care for what is generically called 'big data' and analytical knowledge in personalized medicine. This is also sometimes called P4 medicine, standing for predictive, preventative, personalized and participatory. In the shift, analysing the genome and analysing data relative to therapeutics and effects becomes quite important. Developing the health care, and regulating it, will require the combination and integration of information technology (IT) and specialized medical knowledge about health care applications. The institutional and market context is expected to change dramatically within the next 30 years.

There are reasons for Big Data to find innovative opportunities based upon their extensive technology and foci. In health care, provision will change in fundamental ways towards a system where individuals hold more responsibility, but at the same time, more effort must go into maintaining and monitoring the overall health care system. Individuals will, on the one hand, need to become even more active consumers in preventing medical conditions, in monitoring biological and medical information and in choosing among alternative treatments. Thus, in return, the promise is that the individual can obtain better health benefits. They will be offered specific, individually tailored combinations of pharmaceuticals, health care services, preventative medicine such as exercise and new diets and so forth.

Let us take the example of scenarios for genetic testing for understanding how the business model can differ depending upon the purpose or who pays. There are broadly three contexts in which an individual could access genetic testing or have their whole genome sequenced:

1. Clinical genetic testing. Testing is for the purpose of clinical diagnostic testing and/or population screening. It aims to answer a specific medical question in order to improve diagnosis, prognosis, management and surveillance.
2. Research genetic testing. The primary purpose of testing in a research context is to further biomedical research. Typically, assays are offered to families, groups or sub-populations, with the aim of improving scientific understanding of a particular disease through

genomics and are funded by research funding bodies or commercial companies.

3. Personal genetic testing. Such tests vary widely in purpose, and individuals may order them either with a specific medical concern or driven by curiosity about genomics, disease risk or personal history (such as ancestry or relatedness).

These three contexts are not mutually exclusive, and the boundaries between them are often blurred. However, the three different scenarios entail substantially differing rights and responsibilities on the part of both the genome 'donor' (patient, research participant or customer) and the service provider and other relevant parties.

Paradoxically, on the other hand, this radical push towards individually tailored health care provision requires large quantities of data and new coordination of the overall public and private health care systems and research and development (R&D). Medical researchers and professionals will need information about many variables related to the populations, as well as deeper medical understanding of diseases. This will in turn call for massive public investment into areas like pharmacogenomics, systems biology and bioinformatics, as well as new public-private compromises to access large-scale data and biological material useful as biomarkers, genomic information and others.

A related important question is: who are the customers? Customers include three types of organization: research institute, pharmaceutical company and hospital.

With the advantage of the next-generation sequencing platform and the mass spectrometry platform, the BGI research institute not only provides a variety of solutions for human genetics and diseases research based on a multi-omics strategy (including strategies of genomics, transcriptomics, epigenomics, proteomics and even matagenomics), but also promotes scientific research as well as facilitating applications in molecular breeding, agriculture production and conservation. Big Data is dedicated to providing a systematic, effective and customized solutions to their partners.

To date, Big Data has established collaborations with 15 of the top 20 global pharmaceutical companies since the first project with MSD started in 2010. Big Data are committed to working with customers and collaborators to find creative solutions to the real challenges presented by biopharmaceutical research.

In the health care area, Big Data contributes to genomics research and technology breakthroughs in health care and medicine by cooperation with hospitals. Big Data has developed many detection technologies for public health, such as single-gene mutation disease detection, personal genome sequencing and analysis, HLA high resolution typing, HPV gene typing, non-invasive prenatal genetic testing, HBV gene typing, drug resistant gene detection and many more.

Finally, who are the competitors? Global competitors to Big Data are generally funded by public policy and are generally organized as research institutes. This is as true for health care as for agriculture/food, even if the following examples only focus upon health care.

The Wellcome Trust Sanger Institute was established specifically as a facility for large-scale research. The then Sanger Centre, a joint Wellcome Trust and MRC venture, was set up in 1993 as a new research centre designed to play a role in mapping, sequencing and decoding the human genome and the genomes of other organisms. The Institute has evolved from primarily a sequencing centre to become a leading biomedical research facility. The Wellcome Trust Sanger Institute is now a non-profit organization primarily funded by the Wellcome Trust and run by the charity Genome Research Ltd.

The Broad Institute was founded less than ten years ago, but its history actually goes much further back into successful large-scale scientific collaborations in genomics and chemical biology that grew out of major initiatives at Harvard and MIT, respectively. The Institute's organization is unique among biomedical research institutions. It encompasses three types of organizational units: core member laboratories, programmes and platforms. Scientists within these units work closely together – and with other collaborators around the world – to tackle critical problems in human biology and disease.

Moreover, in addition to the research institutes, some private companies have strong competencies and interest in the health care field. These are usually incumbent firms, especially pharmaceuticals, diagnostics, instruments and medical devices but also in areas related to agriculture.

Amersham (now GE Healthcare) is a world leader in medical diagnostics and in life sciences. 'Our company is focused on enabling molecular medicine, working through three main business areas in diagnostic imaging, protein separations and discovery systems' (http://www. amersham.com). The pre-merge Amersham Pharmacia was an early commercializer of high-throughput sequencers of genetic data developed at the European Molecular Biology Laboratory (EMBL) (Harvey and McMeekin, 2007). Their current aim is to develop personalized medicine centring on diagnostic imaging agents (Amersham Health) and enabling technologies for gene and protein research, drug screening and testing, and protein separations systems (Amersham Biosciences).

GATC is a privately owned company based in Germany. It provides a wide range of sequencing services using both capillary sequencing and next generation sequencing (NGS) for individual DNA samples through to complete genome projects. It also offers a comprehensive bioinformatics service for sequence evaluation. Primarily aimed at present at the industry and academic research sectors, the company clearly has the potential to widen its sphere of interest into the health care sector. It currently has a broad customer base in over 40 countries and subsidiary companies in the UK, France and Sweden.

Complete Genomics is a US company established in 2005 with the specific aim of providing a comprehensive human DNA service for pharmaceutical and academic research. Using high-throughput NGS employing DNA nanoball arrays and combinational probe anchor ligation reads, they provide complete human genome sequencing together with full analysis of the data for use in complete human genome studies. Though specifically aimed at the research market at present, they also have the potential to move into the provision of complete genome sequencing for individuals, or the private and public health care sectors should the demand develop.

Up until recent decades, two business models have been dominant within pharmaceuticals (McKelvey et al., 2004) and biotechnology for human health care (McKelvey, 2008), and this is useful to understand how Big Data can offer useful services, knowledge and technology. The two dominant business models are the classical biotechnology model, which is often an academic spin-off specialized in research and that of the large, vertically integrated company like a pharmaceutical company that tries to incorporate all the R&D, production, regulation and sales in-house.

Within the classical biotechnology model, scientific discoveries and technological inventions have been quickly developed within entrepreneurial firms, usually based upon venture capital. They compete through their specialized scientific knowledge, often sold to large companies, as well as through their flexibility such as quick commercialization, alliances and keeping up to date with scientific and technological breakthroughs. These firms invest heavily in R&D – but often have difficulties making money from their internal knowledge resources.

There is also a second model within the large, vertically integrated company business model in which economies of scale and the use of integrated resources have been characteristic. These firms have integrated everything from R&D to production to marketing and after sales monitoring. They have competed through finding the next 'blockbuster drug' in pharmaceuticals and by having large segments of the market in other industries like medical devices (Amir-Aslani and Negassi, 2006). A very similar trend is visible in agricultural biotechnology.

As these two business models are being challenged, the question arises as to how the KIE firm will continue to design the venture, as it reacts to business opportunities.

14.3   WHAT HAVE WE LEARNED?

This KIE venture is outspokenly focused upon using technology and instruments in order to become a leading player and to reduce costs in sequencing genomes in developing bioinformatics knowledge. They are active in applying that knowledge to the health care and agriculture and food industries. These business opportunities can be exploited because their technology and knowledge may be applied to multiple industries. They try in different ways to combine internal resources to offer goods and services that add value to specific groups of customers (including public ones), and this helps differentiate the firm from its competitors.

In this case, the customers include a wide range of organizations – and 'customer value' may be linked to either basic research or the application of technology. However, there is at the same time fierce competition from globally leading research institutes and private firms, and the capital investment is very high while the returns are uncertain. Given the need for large-scale investment in infrastructure as well as understanding of basic science, the KIE venture has chosen one route, which has led to different organizational forms over time.

Another lesson from this case is that the opportunities are there and opening 'space' for new types of ventures and for new partnerships between public and private actors. Of course, expanding markets no doubt offer the greatest possibilities for growth. The type of analysis offered by Big Data is likely to become increasingly important to health care. But investing in the technological infrastructure is expensive and requires access to financing – including both public and private and including Chinese as well as international grants.

The case study thus raises questions for reflection about doing business in China, but also about how the future will look for the industries related to biotechnology and life sciences. For example, how will the relationship between basic research and commercialization evolve? Will the gap between basic research and commercialization in these industries be smaller in the future?

14.4 QUESTIONS FOR FURTHER REFLECTION

It seems likely that Big Data may well create a very different business model than those of existing competitors. Is this a particularly Chinese model?

Prepare a short case study, analysing how other countries have responded. What were the effects of the 'Big Data Research and Development Initiative' announced by the Obama Administration in March 2012?

NOTE

1. Because Big Data is an extreme case, making it anonymous is virtually impossible. We decided to change the name anyway, in keeping with other chapters in this book, but we still include specific references and use material from interviews.

REFERENCES

Amir-Aslani, A. and S. Negassi (2006), 'Is technology integration the solution to biotechnology's low research and development productivity?', *Technovation*, **26** (5–6), May–June, 273–582.

Baeder, G. and M. Zielenziger (2011), 'China: the life science leader of 2020, 2010 PHG Foundation, next steps in the sequence', available at http://www.monitor.com/tabid/67/ctl/ArticleDetail/mid/691/CID/20101611134152307/CTID/1/L/en-US/Default.aspx (accessed November 2012).

Drucker, P.F. (1994), 'The theory of business', *Harvard Business Review*, September–October, 95–104.

Harvey, M. and A. McMeekin (2007), *Public or Private Economies of Knowledge? Turbulence in the Biological Sciences*, Cheltenham, UK and Northampton, MA, USA: Edward Elgar.

Li, Z., J. Zhang, K. Wen et al. (2004), 'Health biotechnology in China – reawakening of a giant', *Nature Biotechnology*, **22**, Supplement, December, DC13–DC18.

Magretta, J. (2002), 'Why business models matter', *Harvard Business Review*, May, Reprint R0205F.

McKelvey, M. (2008), *Health Biotechnology: Emerging Business Models and Institutional Drivers, Report in the OECD International Futures Project, The Bioeconomy to 2030: Designing a Policy Agenda*, Paris: OECD.

McKelvey, M., A. Rickne and J. Laage-Hellman (2004), *The Economic Dynamics of Modern Biotechnology*, Cheltenham, UK and Northampton, MA, USA: Edward Elgar.

Nature (2010), 'The sequence factory', *Nature*, **464** (4), March, 22–4.

Science (2012), 'China's sequencing powerhouse comes of age', *Science*, **335**, 3 February, 516–19, available at http://www.sciencemag.org/content/335/6068/516.full.pdf (accessed November 2012).

Yanmei, Z. (2012), 'Introspection: the reform of Chinese science and education institution from BGI', available at http://www.stdaily.com/kjrb/content/2012-02/12/content_425367.htm (accessed November 2012).

15. Further developing the ideas

Maureen McKelvey and Astrid Heidemann Lassen

15.1 KNOWING AND DOING KIE

In this book we have presented 13 case studies on knowledge intensive entrepreneurship (KIE) under the three broad sectors of transversal technologies, engineering and software; lifestyle technologies; and human health care and food. Together the case studies show the diversity of KIE as well as how entrepreneurs engage in processes of KIE and how these processes are supported by the broader societal context in reality. The case studies give real-life depth and breadth to the conceptual understanding of KIE presented in the companion book *Managing Knowledge Intensive Entrepreneurship.*

Taken together, this case study book is useful for understanding the 'doing' of creating ventures through this type of entrepreneurship, as illustrated through the case studies and empirical insights, as well as the KIE creation model with the companion book (McKelvey and Lassen, 2013) focusing upon the 'knowing' related to structuring our understanding. The model is found in Chapter 1, Figure 1.1, and is based upon this underlying conceptual framework. Much of the knowledge relevant for a specific firm will be developed when the firm is being started and is up and running. Thus, the entrepreneur and the reader interested in starting a firm will have to balance 'doing' and 'knowing'. By 'doing' we mean engaging practically in actual venture creation processes. By 'knowing' we mean learning through specific empirical examples and case studies as well as general knowledge and tools for evaluating processes and outcomes. Both 'doing' and 'knowing' are vital in helping the reader understand how and why they make good choices in practical action.

This combination of 'knowing' KIE and 'doing' KIE presented through the two books is unusual in the sense that often books focus on either one or the other aspect, while we argue that in fact the two are interdependent if we are to move towards a more useful and insightful understanding of KIE and creation of the desired societal effect through KIE.

15.2   FURTHER DEVELOPING THE IDEAS

In this book, each case study tells a complex history of what happens over time as the firms adapt and change dependent on a combination of internal capabilities and ideas with external opportunities and networks. Each of these insights into the reality of entrepreneurs answers a number of questions, and also pinpoints issues that need to be taken into further consideration be it from a practitioner or academic perspective. In this section, we summarize some of the numerous suggestions for further research that have been identified throughout the book. Most have been addressed in some way in existing research, but more detailed cases and explanations of specific phenomena would be useful. It is our hope that this will inspire the reader to continue his or her studies of the KIE phenomena. The suggestions for further reflections can be used as inspiration for class discussions, Master's theses projects or academic research projects. All levels of discussions and studies are of great importance for knowing as well as doing KIE.

The first topic is the difference between management in KIE ventures and in large firms. Several of the cases address the strategic development of KIE and provide insights into how the management process of new ventures differs substantially from that of larger firms. The suggestions made in this book include focusing on KIE management based on its own merits, not only in comparison to management of large firms, in order to understand better how KIE is affected positively and negatively. The case studies provide insight into how KIE management is highly affected by tensions on multiple levels, such as the example of how to translate scientific, technical and creative knowledge into products and services for a future market. Further understanding of the effect of a number of tensions is important in order to determine how best to stimulate KIE.

Another topic is skills and human resources. One way of developing our understanding of how best to stimulate KIE is discussing how entrepreneurs can best develop the appropriate skill sets to conduct KIE. The case studies reveal the details of how knowledge intensive entrepreneurs are faced with numerous competence demands simultaneously, and how they struggle to handle such demands due to scarce resources. Interesting questions to discuss further in relation to the skills of knowledge intensive entrepreneurs and human resources include, for example, which skills are needed at which stages of the development process of the venture, how such skills are best developed and which roles should universities play in the development of entrepreneurial skills.

A third topic related to the development of the KIE venture is networks and networking. Existing research and practical examples demonstrate that this is one of the most important factors of KIE in terms of being a source of input for the KIE venture creation, a necessary component for the development processes of KIE, and an important mechanism for the implementation and diffusion of knowledge and innovation in society. However, in spite of the fact that the importance of networks is generally agreed upon, what we still need to know more about is how networking should be done. In other words, highly interesting and relevant questions include ones such as: Is it possible to identify success factors that help KIE venture managers to network more efficiently? How do the needs for network and networking change over time as the venture develops? How could public policy best support the changing needs that KIE ventures have for networks? What are the motivations for knowledge intensive entrepreneurs to network and collaborate with different types of partners?

The relationship between KIE more broadly and society forms another large topic. The aspect of diffusion of knowledge and innovation, and the most significant characteristics of KIE, is essentially one of the main reasons for the immense interest in the KIE phenomena, as one of the important ways in which KIE creates growth in society. The case studies address knowledge diffusion in several ways, and also pinpoint aspects that could be very useful to conduct additional research. One is the study of the extent to which entrepreneurs create their new ventures based on previous work experiences, and how this affects the performance of the new ventures.

Another aspect is the long-term effects of KIE created at regional or national levels, including jobs and development of new industries. A common way of analysing the effects of KIE is to focus on the number of firms established. This essentially builds on the assumption that knowledge is tied to the firm – so that if the number of firms increases, so does the knowledge, and if the number of firms decreases, so does the knowledge. However, as demonstrated in several cases in this book, knowledge transcends the individual firm, and is able to cross industrial boundaries. As such, the long-term effects of KIE at regional or national levels should be understood in terms of the effects created by the knowledge. Further discussion of this could, for example, be in relation to positive and negative effects of firm closure in a regional economy, and the extent to which the exit of firms can actually lead to new venture creation through application of knowledge in different contexts.

A better understanding of knowledge and its relationship to growth in society is also crucial for better understanding global relationships as compared to local ones. When looking beyond regional or national economies, we find that the topic of KIE in international settings is highly relevant to analyse further. This book includes case studies on KIE as a part of internationalization processes, as well as case studies on KIE in different international settings, and these highlight some of the differences in how KIE is practised depending on the context. KIE ventures and internationalization processes face an increasingly important issue, which is how to mobilize knowledge and exploit innovative opportunities on a global scale. KIE ventures are to an increasing degree dependent on global knowledge and global resources, and this creates a number of new challenges and opportunities that should be further researched. The case studies on KIE in specific international settings present a picture of KIE as being highly dependent on the political and social ecosystem in which it unfolds. In this relation it could be interesting to further study and compare KIE in different parts of the world; for example, is there a particular Chinese or Indian model of KIE, and how does one best navigate in such a model?

Finally, more research is needed on entrepreneurship in a broader sense. A number of the case studies address KIE in settings not typically emphasized in this type of research, which instead usually focuses upon academic spin-offs and KIE ventures dependent upon science and technology. This book includes a richer range of case studies, including lifestyle technologies, low-tech markets and traditional industries. These case studies illustrate a number of interesting questions related to, for example, what are the primary mechanisms driving such areas, and which kind of knowledge is critical to develop to support KIE in these areas. These case studies illustrate the fruitfulness of exploring KIE in different types of sectors, as well as the role of different types of knowledge in renewing competitiveness in these types of firms.

REFERENCE

McKelvey, M. and A.H. Lassen (2013), *Managing Knowledge Intensive Entrepreneurship*, Cheltenham, UK and Northampton, MA, USA: Edward Elgar.

Index